SYSTEMATIC MARKETING

HOW TO GROW YOUR FIRM WITHOUT LOSING YOUR MIND

Proven Systems to Build a Sales and Marketing Machine
That Will Grow Your Law Practice Without Fail

KEN HARDISON

Systematic Marketing:
How to Grow Your Firm Without Losing Your Mind

—Disclaimer—

While the author has used his best efforts in preparing this book, he makes no representation or warranties with respect to accuracy or completeness of the contents of this book. The advice and strategies contained herein may not be suitable for your situation. You should consult a professional where appropriate. The author shall not be liable for any loss of profit or any other special, incidental, consequential or other damages. The purchaser or reader of this publication assumes responsibility for the use of these materials and information. Adherence to all applicable laws and regulations, both advertising and all other aspects of doing business in the United States or any other jurisdiction, is the sole responsibility of the purchaser of reader.

ISBN-13: 978-0692463895
ISBN-10: 0692463895

Ken Hardison
802 41st Avenue South
North Myrtle Beach, SC 29582
(843) 361-1700
www.pilmma.org

Paperback
Expert
www.PaperbackExpert.com

Table of Contents

Chapter 4

Chapter 5

Introduction

I don't chase ambulances.

I market.

To get here, I had to overcome the hallowed tradition that marketing—or advertising, to use the word all lawyers once despised—was beneath the dignity of the profession.

But as I watched the growth of marketing by lawyers, I rethought the concept. Don't misunderstand me. Plenty of lawyers who advertise are ambulance chasers. But I was better than that.

I analyzed what I did and why I did it. I was trying to help people right a wrong, to better their lives, to find justice, or at least mercy. I was as good a lawyer as any and better than many. If I believed that about myself, shouldn't I let people know I was available? Didn't I have an obligation to inform people about the services I provided and tell them how to find me?

This change in my thinking came in 1993, as lawyers began to advertise heavily on television. I was with the oldest firm—it opened it 1929—in my town, and I discussed advertising with my colleagues. But they concluded, again, that advertising was unprofessional. They would not travel that path.

So I left and opened my own practice. I took an associate and three staff. I learned everything I could and started marketing. Six years later, I had 13 lawyers and 48 staff. We were earning $8 million a year.

This happened because I was willing to think beyond traditional advertising, which, indeed, often was unprofessional or downright sleazy. But I refused to let the well-deserved reputation of the ambulance-chasing lawyers prevent me from offering my services as widely as I could. Why shouldn't I avail myself of a perfectly honorable and time-proven system of offering information to consumers?

So I created a system of marketing and follow-up that changed my life—professionally and personally. I began to attract prospects and convert them into clients by simply thinking about how I would like to be treated as a prospective client and then building those human elements into my system.

I don't chase people down. I educate them and let them come to me. I build trust that persuades them to pick me because they know me and like me.

Years after I started marketing my firm, I had an experience with a plumber that confirmed everything I had come to believe and practice. The lesson seems obvious and simple, but it's a concept we overlook.

I had moved to Myrtle Beach, and I needed a plumber. I found one online with good reviews, so I hired him. He did an excellent job, charged me a reasonable price, left me a business card, and that was the end of our relationship.

Six months later, I needed a plumber for hot-water problems. But I had lost my plumber's business card. I could not remember who this guy was. I searched for him online. Nothing jogged my memory.

So I hired another plumber I found online. He came out, did a great job, and charged me a reasonable price too. But instead of a traditional business card, he stuck a magnet on my water heater. It had his name and contact information. He started sending me his newsletter every three months.

Next time I had a problem, I called him.

My plumber has something that his competition didn't have, something that many lawyers don't have. He has a marketing system. It's not a sophisticated bells-and-whistles operation. It's a system with a simple process, and he backs it up with good work.

Because of his work ethic and his system, he has my business forever.

** *

Soon after I started practicing law, lawyers were spending probably $100 million a year on TV advertising. That number has increased tenfold since I started practicing law; in the past 10 years, it has quadrupled. By the close of 2015, lawyers will have spent more than a billion dollars on TV advertising.

It wasn't always that way. When I hung out my shingle, all we had were Yellow Pages and word of mouth. Then TV came on the scene, and then the web. In those days, lawyers believed that advertising was unprofessional.

In the years after I started with the old-line firm in my town, I built a successful practice by simply wowing clients and cross-selling. No advertising. I was getting better and better. But around 1992-1993, lawyers really started heavily advertising on TV. My business dropped off a little in 1994, even though I was a better lawyer.

I had an epiphany the day one of my former clients—I'll call him Joe—rolled into the courtroom on crutches.

"What happened?" I asked him.

Someone had T-boned him, he said.

"Don't you know I do personal injury?" I asked.

Yes, he said, but he had seen his new lawyer on television: "I figured he must be good at it."

I was stumped. I knew this lawyer. I was winning more cases. I had a good reputation in the personal injury arena. But prospects were calling this lawyer because he was on TV.

When I went back to the office, I told my partners: "We've got to start advertising."

But we didn't, and I opened my new firm, and I learned marketing as I went.

*

Our professors of law taught us how to think, but they did not teach us how to run a business or market our practice. They didn't teach us about marketing, if they even knew the word. My greatest challenge in more than 30 years as a lawyer, therefore, has been to attract clients.

Most lawyers, those who market at all, market haphazardly. You can advertise on Facebook, purchase client lists, utilize Search Engine Optimization or broadcast a TV commercial. But without a plan for attracting, tracking, contacting, and following up, the result is haphazard. You need a system. I wrote this book to teach you what our law schools didn't. Without a system for growing a firm, even the greatest lawyers won't achieve all that they should.

In any business, legal or otherwise, consistency is one of the most important goals. We achieve consistency through *systems*. The marketing system you create—or better yet, the series of marketing systems—will help you to overcome resistance that is inherent in people looking for your service. Your well-designed system will incorporate the processes and procedures for ease of marketing.

Creating the system is the hard part, but once you establish this sales machine, your life will be easier and more rewarding. You will have a consistent flow of new leads and new clients. Your office life will be better. Your home life will be better. Your stress level will drop. You will not have to worry about where the next client is coming from. You can relax because your marketing systems will create a steady flow of leads on a monthly, weekly, and even daily basis.

As a lawyer, you want to practice law. You do not want to spend all of your time on marketing. But without clients, you do not have anyone for whom to practice law! You must get away from hit-or-miss marketing and resist the new shiny gimmick of the week.

In 1996, I read Michael Gerber's book *The E-Myth Revisited*. That was a life changer. I always knew I needed systems for running processes and procedures, for managing the office and for working a case. But I learned that I needed a system to market my practice. And so do you.

In the book you hold in your hands, I will chart your path to a great marketing system that will produce a steady flow of leads and clients. Once you have enjoyed the benefits of systematic marketing, you will never want to go back.

Ken Hardison

June 2015

Chapter 1

Foundations

We are asking people to put their livelihoods and their very lives into our hands, so they must know us, like us, and trust us. People choose and refer lawyers they *know, like,* and *trust.* We market our services so that we can introduce ourselves and establish a level of trust.

In our profession, marketing has been a dirty word, and in the way some lawyers have practiced it, marketing is a dirty business. But there is a better way, an ethical and professional approach that allows us to inform potential clients about an honorable and critical service that can change their life for the better.

We must educate people about our profession, not sell it to them. An educated client who makes an informed decision to hire you will be a more satisfied client than one who feels he was cajoled into the decision. No one likes to be sold to, but everyone likes to buy. If you remember that paradigm as you read, you will better understand my principles and see greater success. Remember: educate, don't sell.

In the end, however, we are asking people to choose our service over another's. Education, then, must involve an element of selling. So you're going to discover how to sell without selling.

The key to win the trust of a person is to put yourself in front of them and give them reasons to like you. Several years ago, Alyn-Weiss & Associates conducted a major survey of consumers regarding TV commercials for lawyers. The purpose of the survey was to learn why so many people don't like commercials for lawyers, especially personal injury lawyers. Alyn-Weiss & Associates found that consumers keyed in on two main qualities when they choose a lawyer to hire: approachability and trustworthiness.

That confirms what I have said for many years: People hire lawyers they know, like, and trust.

Lawyers, of course, have a higher mountain to climb than many other business owners because of the preconception that all lawyers are crooks. That knowledge should clearly convince you that you must create marketing systems that persuade your prospects to know, like, and trust you.

Running the Machine

In one of my previous books, *Under Promise Over Deliver*, I organized marketing systems into three phases:

Before Representation

During Representation

After Representation

Before Representation is the phase on which most lawyers focus. They want to advertise to find new leads, whether online, TV, pay-per-click, newspaper, direct mail, or any other medium. But the other two phases are as critical to success as the first.

During Representation you must focus on exceeding expectations. This is the time you fully satisfy your client and earn his loyalty. In *Under Promise Over Deliver*, I further discuss the Theory of Preeminence, which is neither new nor my invention. Jay Abraham—a marketing guru and one of my mentors—talks about this theory at length. Basically, the theory states: "Everything you do should be for the betterment of your client."

Lawyers take an oath to do that, but with our own bills to pay, families to tend to, and needy clients, we neglect this very simple rule. But we can't forget it. It's a core value at the center of many ethical systems: Treat people the way you want to be treated.

When you follow this core value, you create an atmosphere of trust. People will like you so much that they become raving fans. You want to "Wow!" them so that they go out and become your own little mini-marketers. Merely demonstrating your adequacy is not enough—you must exceed your clients' expectations. We are in a service business, and it's not just about legal services. Our work is about *client* service—meeting their needs when they come to us with problems. Every person who comes to a lawyer has a problem. We exist to solve that problem.

We can get so caught up in the legal part of our practice that we forget that these people are human beings and need to be treated as such. If you instill this ethic in every member of your firm, you will receive referrals upon referrals. Believe it or not, there are systems for referrals—I'm going to share those with you later. You can create marketing systems for your clients so that they will refer you to their families and friends. Remember: People refer to lawyers they know, like, and trust.

The third phase, After Representation, is the phase that 98 percent of lawyers forget or ignore because they are more occupied with finding new leads than remembering their established clients.

The truth is that a referral from an established, satisfied client requires far less effort than converting a new lead from the large pool of potential clients who don't know you, what you do, or what you stand for. With cold prospects, you have to create the "know, like, and trust" from nothing.

In contrast, your existing clients already know, like, and trust you—and that is what they will tell those they refer. Invest in the After Representation phase and leverage the clients with whom you already have relationships.

Marketing systematically in these three phases is so much easier and so much cheaper than traditional haphazard marketing. There are so many tactics and systems that you can create in your law firm that will bring you new business. Through a holistic approach to the three phases of marketing in which you develop marketing systems for each phase, you will find incredible success. From my personal experience, I can tell you that it is truly unbelievable. The creation of your system is hard work, and you are not going to create it overnight. So simply tackle it the same way you eat an elephant—one bite at a time.

Chapter 2

You Must Stand Out From the Clutter

You Need a USP

The variety of marketing systems I will share with you have a common goal: To make you stand out from the clutter, by which I mean the daily deluge of advertisements. Estimates suggest that advertisers assault us with anywhere from 3,000 to 300,000 ads each day. The result is that one business looks just like every other business. With the Internet, Facebook ads, pay-per-click ads, email blasts, television commercials, radio spots, and more, it has become increasingly difficult for consumers to distinguish between competing firms. The problem for law firms is worse than for most other professions—people seem to think that all law firms are equal.

Every day, your competitors hammer prospects with hundreds of ads that say the same things: "We're tough and aggressive." "We care." "Free Consultation." "We don't get paid unless we win." These ads clutter the airwaves and have consumers' heads spinning. No wonder prospective clients don't know whom to hire—no one stands out!

You can rise above the clutter with one simple concept, and failure to use this is a mistake you make with every advertising dollar that you spend.

What is the concept?

A USP.

A USP is a Unique Selling Proposition—a simple statement of benefits that differentiates you from your competition. The majority of lawyers assume that they can compete by copying their competitors' ads. Even though imitation is the sincerest form of flattery, when it comes to marketing your law firm and beating your competition, it falls flat. Don't fall into this trap. This is ineffective, costly, and offers you no advantage whatsoever.

You need a USP.

Rosser Reeves introduced the concept in his 1961 book, *Reality in Advertising*, and revolutionized the marketing industry. The book was so influential that it became a college textbook for marketing students. Mr. Reeves wrote that every business, product, or service absolutely must have a Unique Selling Proposition. A well-defined USP, he wrote, is the key to creating an effective and cohesive advertising and marketing campaign that will set you apart from the other law firms in your market.

Simply put, a USP is:

- An overt, unique claim about your law firm or a promise of the benefits you offer a client.

- A statement that impressively positions you as distinctly different from your competitors.

- A statement that is so strong, attractive, and compelling that it motivates prospects to choose your firm over all others.

A USP answers two basic questions:

❶ *Why should I hire a lawyer at all?*

And:

❷ *Why should I do business with your law firm rather than with your competitors?*

How can a prospective client choose the right law firm when they all look the same, sound the same and make all the same promises? The fact that the legal advertising space is cluttered with cookie cutter ads is actually a good thing for you. This gives you a golden opportunity to stand out from your competition.

So develop a USP. Now.

How to Develop Your Firm's USP

Most lawyers I talk to say, "Ken, we do all the same things our competitors are doing." "We are bound by laws and regulations on what we can do and what we can say to potential clients." "We don't have much of a choice. There really is no way to stand out from the crowd."

My answer to that is simply: You can do it. It isn't easy, but with the right mindset and tools, you can create a USP that will increase the return on your investment (ROI) from your advertising three times to 10 times your current yield.

You may already have one and just don't know it. Think about it—do you provide a particular benefit that all other lawyers in your market similarly provide or offer but no one promotes it because everyone else provides it? So what if everyone else does it? If no one is promoting it, you should be the first to shout it from the rooftops! Let it set you apart. This is called a pre-emptive USP.

Although all the other lawyers do the same thing, you will give yourself a competitive advantage simply by stating it.

If you are the first lawyer to advertise that "We will handle your Personal Injury or Med Pay Claim for free," people will perceive you as the market leader. Consumers will view the firms that follow suit with the same claim as "copycats" and "me-too" firms. The copycats will only end up advertising you.

What Do Your Ads Say About You?

McGraw Hill Publications ran a memorable ad many years ago that was so good that I had to include it here for you. A grumpy old man stares out at you from the ad, saying:

I don't know who you are.

I don't know your company.

I don't know your company's product.

I don't know what your company stands for.

I don't know your company's customers.

I don't know your company's record.

I don't know your company's reputation.

Now—what was it you wanted to sell me?

The moral of this, as the ad concludes, is that "Sales start before your salesman calls…" Or in the case of your law firm, before you talk to the potential client. Here's the deal—clients do not care about you or your law firm. They don't care how long you've been in business or how great you are. All they care about is themselves and the all-important questions: "What's in it for me? How will I benefit from your services?"

To develop a powerful and effective USP, you must think like a potential client. What keeps them up at night? What is their big problem you can solve?

To sell you must compel. The selling starts with your ads.

There are three primary ways to properly develop a USP for your firm. If you take the time to work through the following three exercises, you will have the basics of a USP to polish and shine until it sparkles like a diamond and attracts all sorts of new clients. By seeking to find your perfect USP and completing these exercises, you will have taken the proactive route. Creating a compelling USP is one of the most powerful things you can do for your law firm.

Don't try to do these exercises in your head. It's imperative that you get a pen and paper and write everything down! For the first exercise, it would be best if you could do it with a friend or a group of colleagues—when it comes to a USP, the more minds the better! You never know what a staff member, a friend or a family member may come up with. You may be too close to it to really hone in on what you need to say.

The second and third exercises require you to interact with your clients. Who better to help you craft a USP than those who are intimately aware of you and your services and how they can benefit people? Why did they choose you? What were some of the fears they had about dealing with attorneys? How do they feel about your competitors' ads? All of this information will be beneficial to the USP creation process.

But before you go there, let's start with the first exercise. Take out a pen and a notepad, close the door, turn off the TV, and get ready to work through these three exercises.

The Gary Halbert Index Card Shuffle

The only way to truly answer a potential client's most critical question, "What's in it for me?", is to sell the "benefits" of your law firm and not the "features" of your legal services.

What's the different between a benefit and a feature?

Take the eraser on a pencil for example. The feature of that eraser is that it will erase your mistakes. The eraser benefits you by saving you time and effort by not requiring you to rewrite everything from the beginning if you make a mistake. The benefit is the time you save. See the difference?

How about a benefit versus a feature in a USP?

Let's take Domino's Pizza. They advertise "Piping Hot Pizza Delivered in 30 minutes or less…" The benefit is hot, instead of cold, pizza, and fast, instead of slow, delivery. By focusing on the benefits, the company is showing the consumers what's in it for them. Every consumer now knows if you order Domino's, you'll get hot pizza delivered fast. This is how Domino's differentiated itself from its competitors and created a multimillion-dollar business.

Domino's never claimed to be the best-tasting pizza. They focused on their target market—people who wanted pizza fast and cheap. Focus on your prospective clients. What do they want? Your USP should tell them that you're the firm that can give it to them better than any other. This is key. You must know what your prospective clients want in order to create a USP that works.

One of the best ways to hash out your firm's features versus benefits is to use the Gary Halbert Index Card Shuffle, popularized by the famous copywriter Gary Halbert. He writes a service feature on one side of an index card and then, on the other side, turns that feature into a benefit.

How do you turn features into benefits?

Simply use the methods I'm about to teach you, and you'll nail it every time.

Each time you consider one of your service features, put yourself in your client's shoes and ask, "So what? What's in it for me? What does that do for me?"

Answer those questions for each and every service feature and design your USP around the ways you serve your clients better than everyone else. Fulfilling their needs and satisfying their desires is the key to growing your business.

What you will offer your clients are benefits. BIG BENE-FITS. Benefits galore! And you'll do this as you answer the question: "What's in it for me?" You will have turned features into benefits. Benefits are what clients want.

After you finish writing a whole stack of cards, one for each feature/benefit combination, flip through and rank them. Select the strongest, most powerful, or most unique benefit, and put that card at the top of your deck.

Then prioritize the benefits in terms of what's most important to the marketplace, hardest for a competitor to duplicate, or what you do best. Every situation is different, so prioritize accordingly, taking the particular circumstances of your market into account. Next, sort and arrange the remaining cards in descending order based on their ranking assigned during prioritization.

The most powerful benefit should become the cornerstone of your USP and the headline on any ad you run. The remaining benefits should become subheadings throughout your advertising copy.

Frustration vs. Satisfaction

Why do people resist hiring a lawyer? Many lack the money or are afraid the lawyer will take advantage. I used this fear to create the USP for my own law firm. We use a *"30-Day Client Service Satisfaction Guarantee—No questions and no fees."* We give new clients the opportunity to try our firm for 30 days. At any time during the first 30 days, if they aren't completely 100 percent satisfied with the way we treat them and their case, they can ask for their file back with no fees.

(See www.CarolinaSSDLawyers.com.)

The benefit of this compelling offer is that the potential client can "try us" and change lawyers without the fear of having to pay a second lawyer if they aren't 100 percent happy. In our USP, I incorporated the concept of risk reversal. By giving them a 30-Day Guarantee with no fees, we assume all of the risk, leaving the client able and willing to take action risk-free.

The concept of capitalizing on frustration versus satisfaction leads me to the second method for creating your USP, which has been popularized by marketing guru Dan Kennedy, one of the brightest marketing minds in the world.

Why don't people want to hire a lawyer?

Ask them.

Bring your clients into the mix.

Basically, you want to find out what keeps potential clients from hiring a lawyer. What are they most dissatisfied with regarding your type of service. In other words, what do they care about most? Whatever it is, make the point that you have solved these issues squarely in the middle of your USP. Tell potential clients that you have fixed the problems most clients have with lawyers, and they will beat a path to your door.

To sharpen your point, find out what is less than perfect about law firms in your practice area. Then, rid your firm of those imperfections and advertise the fact that you've addressed those issues and solved those problems.

Ask a few of your clients these questions:

What is your greatest frustration about dealing with insurance companies?

What is your biggest worry in dealing with the Social Security administration?

What's the thing you hate most about dealing with your employer when you've been hurt?

Why do you really hate coming to a lawyer?

The answers will tell you exactly what the clients want because you'll know what they don't want. You are basically asking people what's missing in the marketplace and then supplying it.

Many lawyers are too close to their own firms and think they know everything about them, including what their clients want. Therefore they are hesitant, stubborn, afraid, and unwilling to ask their clients what they think. This is a huge mistake. You must ask them. You are not your client. If you try to give your clients something they don't want or something you think they want without asking, and they go for it, you will just be a lucky lawyer. If they don't go for it, you will have wasted all that time and effort.

The key thing to remember when developing a USP is this: *You can't be all things to all people.* Select your USP and stick with it. You should use it in everything you do to market and advertise your firm. It should become your mantra—and you should use the heck out of it! It is, after all, who you are.

Most lawyers say, "We all do the same things and are constrained by rules and regulations, so our hands are tied." I disagree. *What* you do may be the same, but *how* you do it is a different consideration altogether. You could have a "Client Bill of Rights" or a Client Advocate. You could offer to handle property damage for free. You could fold all these things into your USP.

Uncover Your Hidden USP—Why You?

This third exercise will solidify the foundation you established with the first two exercises and will give you the tools you need to complete the construction of your USP.

Here's what you do:

First, list the 50 clients who send you the most referrals. They are your best clients. They are your raving fans. These are the people you want to learn more about. Why did they hire you? What is it about your firm that made them choose you?

Ask these clients to complete these sentences for you:

The main reason I chose your law firm was _____

_____.

The one word that stands for your law firm is _____

_____.

Every other law firm does _____ while you do

_____.

The first thing that comes to mind when I think of your law firm or you personally is _____.

Your law firm is unique and special because _____

_____.

The one thing you do well is _____

_____.

The first time I tried your law firm I thought _____

_____.

I always refer clients to you because _____

_____.

The biggest problem with your law firm is _____

_____.

If only your law firm would _____

_____ instead of _____.

Your firm is where it is today because of _____

_____.

Your current clients are a wonderful resource who usually will offer honest answers about your firm. You can use their insights as valuable testimonials and endorsements in your marketing efforts. When you receive positive feedback, ask the clients for permission to share their remarks.

Once you've created your USP, polish it and use it everywhere. With a little bit of work and perhaps some help from your staff, clients, friends, or even marketing associates, you might be able to reduce a 30-word or 40-word USP into just 10 words or even just one or two lines. Your USP should say everything without saying too much. Short and concise, but not too short.

You'll know it's right when you've got a complete and compelling statement that sets you apart from your competition.

Once you have created your Unique Selling Proposition, you have to convey it to your target audience. If you're a domestic lawyer, you need to communicate your USP to people who are experiencing marital difficulties. If you serve clients who have been in car wrecks, you must transmit your USP to them. Your message has to stand out from all of the clutter. The key to accomplishing that standout effect and communicating your USP to these markets is quite simple: write great advertisements.

You Must Write Great Advertisements

Creating good advertisements is truly an art and a science. You as a lawyer probably don't want to understand everything about advertisements, but you need to hire someone who does understand it. Even if you are not the one who oversees your firm's advertisements, as a minimum you need to understand each of the following components of a great advertisement.

Create the Headline

The first component of a great advertisement is the headline. I probably spend more time on headlines than on any other part of the ad, because if you do not arrest your prospects' attention immediately, they are going to bypass you. When I create an ad, I might write 30 to 50 different headlines. Using free-flow thinking, I record whatever comes to mind, no matter how outrageous. My central focus is grabbing each prospect's attention.

One way to capture attention is to include numbers. Of all the different advertisements that I have tested, those with headlines like "The Three Things You Must Do Before Filing for a Divorce" or "The Five Things You Should Never Tell a Police Officer During a Traffic Stop" tend to perform the best. You want to write engaging headlines like those, because if your headline is uninteresting, your prospect will stop reading and miss your message.

Another way to write an excellent headline is to enter the conversations that are already going on inside people's minds. You can enter those conversations by paying attention to popular current events. These ads are only good as long as the current event is in the news, but while they last, this approach is effective.

For example, I wrote an advertisement for PILMMA before a Super Bowl. The New England Patriots were going to play, and there was a big commotion about deflated footballs. Bob Kraft is the owner of the Patriots, and one of the members of PILMMA is also named Bob Kraft. So I put his name into the ad headline and played off that throughout. It was an incredibly successful advertisement.

Write the Body

To write the body of your advertisement, you want to figure out what is keeping people awake at night. What problems do they have? Agitate those problems, even make them seem worse, and then present your solution.

Make sure your ad is focused on the reader. Every time I visit a new city, I pull out the local Yellow Pages and look at the advertisements from lawyers. Invariably, the advertisements fail to realize that the reader is concerned about one question: "What's in it for me?"

Your advertisements must answer that question. The prospect really doesn't care much about you, except insofar as you can assist him. When you are writing the copy for your ad, count the number of times you mention "I" and "we" and "us." Eliminate as many first-person pronouns as you can and say "you" and "your" instead. Focus on "you, your family, your wife, your justice, etc."

When you present your service, remember to stress benefits and not features. People buy the benefits of your service (what *they* receive), not the features (what you do).

Ensure that all of your advertisements are clear and easy to understand. Always write on a 5th- to 7th-grade level.

Include a strong call to action in every single advertisement. By "call to action," I do not mean that you must literally instruct the prospect to pick up the phone, although that is an example of an effective call to action. The action can be any sort, whether filling out a form, calling a recorded phone line to hear a message, opting in online to receive a white paper, or requesting a free book. A call to action motivates people to act.

Once I have written my ad, I ask non-lawyers to look at it. I don't let other lawyers look at my advertisements. If a lawyer likes one of my ads, then it's probably no good. In my business, the target demographic is primarily comprised of ordinary blue-collar workers, not lawyers.

This information has a broader application than just advertising. In fact, these strategies are key in developing any sort of message or content. That is why I chose to share information about Unique Selling Propositions and content creation before I delved into the details of the marketing systems: These two matters are foundational.

You can create all the marketing systems in the world, but if you don't have a USP, or have the wrong message, you will severely limit the effectiveness of the systems. Conversely, the right USP and the right message breathe life into any marketing system.

We have talked about the foundation and about what you must do to stand out from the clutter. Now we are going to turn a corner and lay out the practical blueprint.

Chapter 3

How to Properly Handle a New Lead

We talked about laying the foundation so that you can start building your sales machine. Now I will give you the blueprint. The Number One key to this is: You've got to track a lead and then capture it. To do this, you need a system. In our marketing systems, we're not about selling. We're about educating prospects and then nurturing them. We educate them with free reports, videos, and books, and this nurturing is what builds trust.

The system is set up to track, capture, nurture, and convert prospects into new clients. But unless you have built your infrastructure, all this work will be for nothing. You may end up doing more harm than good.

A lawyer once called me after he had settled a big case. In order to offset his tax liability, he wanted to spend half a million dollars on marketing. After I spent a couple days with him, I refused to give him any advice because he hadn't established his infrastructure.

"I could get your phone ringing off the hook," I told him, "but you couldn't handle it. You don't have any infrastructure or any kind of system set up to take in these leads. You don't have the right staff. You don't have any scripts for training. You don't have software or an adequate phone system."

He got very upset with me, but he took my advice. It took him about six months to implement it. I went back to help him create a marketing system, and his business is flourishing now.

So what are some key components of a solid infrastructure?

You need enough phone lines so that callers don't get a busy signal. Your staff, whether the employee is a dedicated intake person or a receptionist, must be trained to "wow" your prospects.

The most important employee in your office is the receptionist, because that's the first voice, the first person that a new client or new lead will talk to or see when he calls or walks into your office. It is a mistake to staff your front desk on the cheap.

You need the proper software. If you go from five leads to 30 leads or 50 leads a week, you better have software that will keep up. I use Infusionsoft, but there's also Avvo Ignite and Captorra. You can even use your case management system.

What are you going to do with calls that come in after business hours and on the weekends and holidays? Some lawyers just forget about them.

The great thing about this machine is it runs 24/7. It's going to be there when you're not in the office, and that's the beauty of the whole marketing system. All this stuff is done automatically while you're at home sleeping.

This also gives you more time face-to-face with your prospects and clients rather than time spent marketing.

Once you have captured a prospect's contact information, you want to see him within 24 hours. A prospect doesn't want to hear that you can see him in two weeks. He's thinking, "My problem's right now! It's not two weeks from now."

Even if you can't see him right away, you should get him into your office, even if it's just to meet with a paralegal, and get the ball rolling.

These people are seeking a lawyer because they've got a problem. Something is keeping them awake at night. If you don't get to them within 24 hours, they're going to call somebody else.

Once they come into your office and fill out the appropriate paperwork, their search is probably over. We actually did a study on this several years ago. The longer we waited, the more prospects we lost. We gave them time to change their mind or for someone to steer them to another lawyer.

I get to them within 24 hours because I want them to stop looking. I want to start working on the problem. I want to allay their fears and frustrations.

Faster is better. If you take prospects online, two hours isn't soon enough to respond. When it's online, and you get an inquiry form from a prospect, you need to respond within five minutes.

In this age, with everything zipping across the world in 2.1 seconds, you must be on top of things.

How to Track Leads

You have written a great headline and attracted a prospect. Your ad persuades a prospect that you might have the solution for their problem.

Then you have to address the action you want the prospect to take. Let's say that the desired action is to fill out the form on the Internet, on your landing page or your home page. I recommend you use what's called a double opt-in. The reason you want to do this is to verify that you get a good email address from them. Some people will just fill out your form using a bogus email address and then they get your information.

With a double opt-in system, prospects must give you a valid email address. Then your system will send them an email with a link to click for them to access the free report. If they don't give you the proper email, of course, they are not going to get the link. If they really want it, they are going to have to give you the correct information.

Capturing contact information is a must, whether that's from an opt-in form, or you actually pick up the phone and call, or if they register for a webinar or a seminar, or ask for a free book. Through your system, you determine what information you want prospects to give you and if you will deliver your material by physical mail or call them to download it.

When prospects contact you online, getting a first name and email address on a form is sufficient. If they call, you want to get everything you can because they have taken the time to call you, and they are serious.

When you have a system in place, your receptionist, or whoever answers the phone, has a process in place to get all that relevant contact information. That is part of your machine. I don't want people to think that the system is just software. It's the people and the scripts they use. This is how you convince a prospect that you are the preeminent attorney so that they will choose you. One way to do this is to reinforce that they made the right choice. In my new caller script, I get my people to say, "You made the right choice to call us today."

Once you have this information, you can begin the process of educating them. Tell them about the pitfalls associated with their type of case (you'll know this by which ad and landing page they come into your system through), why they need an expert lawyer, and why you are the logical choice. You can do all this without selling. Remember, you are educating.

The system can be as simple as a pad with a different colored paper on it with a different form for new leads. It could be that simple. Or it can be something as sophisticated as Infusionsoft software.

The key is, no matter who's in the office when a prospect calls, the person talking to the prospect must know what to do: Step 1, Step 2, Step 3.

Your employee has a script and is going to know how to be empathetic. When you train your staff, role-play different situations, so that you know that your employees are going to convey the right message. Ghost calls are useful for this training. This happens when you can ask someone you know to call in and act as if they were a prospect.

(If you record all your incoming calls, check your state laws regarding disclosure that you are recording. You might need to say that the call is being recorded for training purposes.)

Follow-Up is the Holy Grail of Conversions

Testimonials

Once you have converted them from a searcher to a prospect, you now want to begin the follow-up process. This is where you educate them and woo them to choose you.

Many times, we'll call this process a nurturing campaign because we are nurturing the relationship and getting them to know, like, and trust us. What you send them in this stage can be as much or as little as you want. We like to make a big impression on them by sending what we call a "shock and awe" package.

This package (which is mailed to them physically) could be stuffed full of as much information as you have available. Information about their type of case, and about you and your firm, and why you are the best choice for them. Be sure to include a few testimonials from previous clients.

I know that in some states, you can't use testimonials in your advertising. But at this point, this is no longer advertising. They have requested information from you.

Testimonials are gold. But I don't call them testimonials. I say, "Here is what people are saying about us." Your wording is important.

I produce a testimonial sheet as part of my shock and awe package. I put the testimonials on the front page and give as much detail as possible without intruding on a client's privacy. The more detail you can give, the better. I include a photograph, the name and hometown. I've seen some lawyers who put in just a blurb and then the client's initials. That's really not enough information as some people won't believe that is a real testimonial. They may think you made it up. You want to make every message relevant, useful, and believable.

In my testimonials I want to include a diverse cross-section of the population. I typically use a testimonial from an African-American male and female, someone of Asian descent, perhaps someone in the military, an older person, and a younger person. Variety is the key as you want to make a connection with the people you serve.

When they do that, they'll like you better and feel that you might be a good person to represent them as well. When prospects connect with one of your past clients, they are more likely to see you as a good fit for their cases.

I'm trying to give them what is called "social proof." As I'm nurturing them I'm also trying to build trust. They're more likely to hire me if they trust me, right? Remember: There is a purpose behind everything you do.

Dealing with Objections and Rejections

Prospects in search of a lawyer will raise many objections. With your USP and materials, you want to put to rest as many fears as possible before they become objections. In this chapter, I will offer strategies that you build into your machine to handle objections.

When you anticipate and prepare for prospects' objections, you can respond and minimize them. It's like your closing argument when you go first. Talk about the pink elephant in the room and take the wind out of their sails first.

Price is almost always one of the concerns. But don't let that tempt you to sell yourself as the cheapest lawyer. You never want to differentiate yourself based on price. Look what happened to K-Mart and Circuit City. You will never win when you differentiate yourself only on price.

You've got to go in there and explain all the things you do that the other lawyers don't. I don't want clients who price shop, because they usually give me the most problems.

When a prospect tells me I'm too expensive, I tell them about the first house I built. I got bids from three builders. My father told me to hire the most expensive one, because he was the master builder. I thought I couldn't afford him, so I hired the cheaper guy. Halfway through the construction, I had to fire the guy and hire the master builder. Ended up costing me more than if I had hired the master builder to begin with.

Early in my career, when I was doing criminal law, I was the most expensive DWI lawyer in town. I was very successful and built a very profitable practice. Prospects would come in and say, "Well, Joe down the road is willing to take my case for $500." I was charging $2,500. I'd look at them and say, "You know, that's the lawyer you probably should call if all you are interested in is a low price.

I tell people all the time that if they are shopping by price, I'm probably not their guy. You get what you pay for.

Three Follow-Up Systems You Must Implement

Your follow-up systems can be simple or complex. But here are three systems that you must put in place.

From prospect calls, I have learned that there are three primary reasons people won't hire me on the first call.

1. They want to do it themselves.

2. They want to talk to a spouse, father figure, sibling, or someone else before they decide.

3. They want to get a top-level attorney, and they're not sure I'm the guy.

Knowing this, I have created three different follow-up systems, depending on which objection they present. These systems include emails, videos, physical mailings, books, phone calls, and a variety of other items. Now I didn't have all of this in place at the beginning, but I've built these systems over time. Start where you are and get some systems in place. It makes everything much easier and will help you open more cases.

There's a process to the system. We have a checklist to ensure everything gets done every time. Different people are doing different things. One employee sends out a card. Another is sending out the emails. I made videos that pop out on these emails. Whatever their objection, I'm addressing it. I'm not selling. I am giving them information to overcome those objections.

If I'm doing a video in which I tell them the story about building my first house, I want it to be personal. People like stories, they can understand that, and they relate to me better. It's all about being different and standing out from the crowd.

Follow-Up Systems Help You Stand Out

Most lawyers' follow-up systems include only a letter they mail out advising you of the statute of limitations on an action and that you may have rights to pursue. That's not follow-up in my book.

I open with a letter that applauds a prospect for searching for a lawyer. Then I offer them questions that they should ask a lawyer before hiring them. I wrote a report on "Eight Questions You Should Ask a Lawyer," and the answers to those questions all point back to me so that I am the obvious choice.

Using Automation

Automation is the facet of your system that cuts your costs. If I spend more than $300 to get a case in the door, I'm not going to make the profit that I want to make. The margins are not going to be high enough.

To cut the cost per new prospect, I put together a 30-minute infomercial in which I am interviewed about my book. When a prospect calls the number on the infomercial, they hear a recording that says: "Hello, I'm glad you called. I'd like to send you a free copy of my book. Please leave your name and address, and I'll mail it to you."

The system then sends me an email when they leave their message. It also goes to one of my administrators, who puts the information into our system and mails the book. I use a company called Automated Marketing Solutions. The cost is 39 bucks a month.

After three days, we call to make sure the book arrived and to ask them whether they have any questions. Three days after that, we call again to ask whether they would like a copy of the report for people who apply for Social Security (or for whatever type of information they are requesting).We then send that out if they would like. We then call back to make sure the report arrived. We give them another chance to ask questions. We suggest that if they have questions that aren't covered in the book or the report, they should talk to one of our lawyers by requesting a free consultation in our office.

Are you starting to see how this follow-up system works to educate them, build trust, and then motivate them to meet with us? Once you set it up properly, the system does the work for you, automatically. This graphic visually explains our infomercial mailing sequence. Each of the next steps is already predetermined, which makes follow-up much easier.

We also put prospects on our list so they will receive our print newsletter, which is nothing like most lawyers send out—if they send anything at all. Seventy-five percent of the newsletter is about me, our staff, and what's going on in the community—it's personal and relationship oriented. Only 25 percent is about law. I'm trying to get them to know me and like me. I'm trying to personalize it. I'm trying to create that relationship. In the process, I can change the prospect's perception of lawyers and of my firm.

CAROLINA DISABILITY
LAWYERS

Infomercial Mailing Sequence

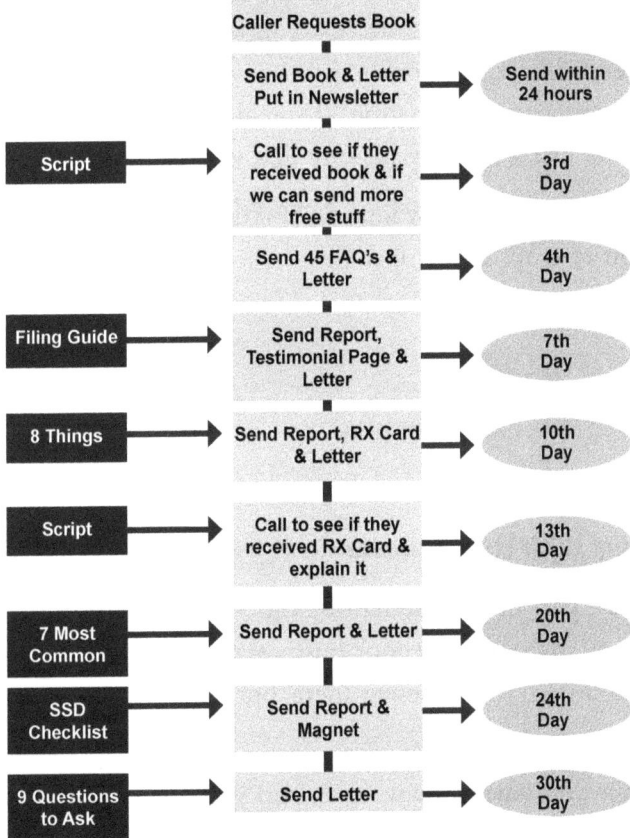

	Caller Requests Book	
	Send Book & Letter Put in Newsletter	Send within 24 hours
Script	Call to see if they received book & if we can send more free stuff	3rd Day
	Send 45 FAQ's & Letter	4th Day
Filing Guide	Send Report, Testimonial Page & Letter	7th Day
8 Things	Send Report, RX Card & Letter	10th Day
Script	Call to see if they received RX Card & explain it	13th Day
7 Most Common	Send Report & Letter	20th Day
SSD Checklist	Send Report & Magnet	24th Day
9 Questions to Ask	Send Letter	30th Day

I know that half of these people are not going to hire me. But with the system, I greatly increase my percentages. Once I make the video, I'm good. Once I create the eight questions, I'm good. Once I create the report or the book, I'm good. It pretty much runs itself, and I'm paying other people much less than what my time is worth to take care of all the details and ensure these systems are running properly. This is my sales machine.

When I started out, I sent out one email. That was my system. But as I encountered different objections, I categorized them into the most common areas and tailored emails to the objections. Then I added those emails to my system. That's how you build the system.

I also sent notes that ask: "Do you want to reach out to a lawyer? Let us know. We don't mean to harass you. We're just trying to give you great information. If you already have a lawyer, that's great. We just want to make sure that you're protected."

People ask me: "How long do you do it?" You do it until they ask you to stop. Remember this, "The more you tell, the more you sell."

Increasing Conversions

Convert With Your Website

A critical part of your system is your website. It's a must! Don't think you can use a Facebook business page or anything else. You can't. You need to be present there, but you must have your own website.

Once you have your website, and you attract good traffic to

your website, you need to convert your visitors into clients. Once prospects raise their hands to say they are interested, you must take the action that moves them to actually say: "I want you to be my lawyer."

As you attract prospects, however, you need to be careful that you don't overwhelm them with information. Lawyers spend thousands of dollars on pay-per-click advertising, which sends prospects to their websites. When prospects go there, they see all the services a lawyer offers, and the clutter scares them off.

Instead, I prefer to use a simple and focused landing page that is the destination from a pay-per-click headline. This page is tailored to the ad they just saw and clicked on. It's the next logical step for them and provides them with more information. The ad may say: "Do you need a will?" The prospect clicks the ad and lands on my page about wills. They will see my offer of a free report or a free book. They can watch a two-minute video. I'm educating them and offering them an opportunity to gain even more information. Remember, the more you tell, the more you sell.

You can fine-tune this system through split-testing, which will tell you which of your approaches are most effective at attracting prospects. In a split test, every other prospect who clicks on your pay-per-click ad goes to a different landing page. You might have a video on one and no video on another one. Or you might use a different word that invites a prospect to opt in: "Click here now for your free report" versus "Download instantly." You test different colors. People act based on psychological triggers, and some things work better than others. You don't know until you test it. Always remember that marketing is a series of tests.

Once you have set up a "control" site, you measure results and can easily tell which landing page performs the best. You just keep testing. You want to increase your conversions per click because you want to limit or decrease your cost per case. One word of caution: Change only one thing at a time so you know whether it works better.

Marketing is a process. You don't set up the system then say, "Okay, it's done. I never have to touch it again." You're always tweaking. You set up a marketing system and review it every 30 days or 60 days to see how it is performing. Then you make one change and monitor it again. This is the true sign of a successful marketer.

Our society is more online than offline now. Fifty percent of Internet searches are done from phones now. And the Internet is not just for people younger than 50. We do Social Security, and we're getting clients in their 50s or 60s. Or people find us because they're searching online on behalf of their parents or grandparents. Online is where it's at for lawyers now.

We have a web-chat program that launches a window when someone is on our website. They can ask a question on the spot. This is instantaneous and makes a big difference. People have lots of questions and if you can give them multiple ways to find answers, you are more likely to gain their business.

We have found when we live chat with someone on our website, our conversions increase another 15 to 20 percent. We make it easy, which is the most important aspect of all of our marketing. A lot of people have problems, and they want answers right now. Live chat is a great solution.

The most significant benefit of having live chat and other interactive elements on your website is that you cut your bounce rate, which is a figure that represents the percentage of visitors to a particular website who navigate away from the site after viewing only one page. You want people to stay on your site and view multiple pages. A high bounce rate is not good. You are not engaging with them. This tells you a lot about your website, your message and the media you are using to get them to your website. You need to know and monitor your bounce rate if you are going to convert more prospects to clients.

Google Analytics will tell you how much time each viewer spends on the site. You want to get that bounce rate as low as you can. The more interesting your site, the longer a prospect will stay on it.

Be careful, however, that you don't make it *too* busy. If you include too much, you create clutter, and your site is ineffective. I learned that the hard way. I had to go back to my site and clean it up. To include too much information is as bad as providing too little. A better approach is to include the additional information in a free report, or better, your own book.

You need to design your website so that your key information is "above the fold," to use an old newspaper term. That means at the top of the page, above the crease where the newspaper is folded. When prospects click to your site, you want your most important information to be the first thing they see on their screen. If they have to scroll down the page, your information is too low. They can scroll down for more information, but your most important information needs to be up top.

I always put my call to action above the fold. I only have three seconds to snag a prospect before they bounce to another site. Keep it simple and dramatic above the fold: "Free Book: The 7 Mistakes People Make in Car Accidents in North Carolina." That'll grab their attention.

People who are searching for information about lawyers will search at all hours. On the web, I am available at 1 o'clock on Monday morning or on Saturday at 8 p.m. People want information when *they* want information. Make sure you have systems in place to provide information 24/7. Ninety percent of your competition is not doing this. Believe me, I've talked with many of them.

I have Mastermind members from all over the country who have built websites and systems like this. It works in North Carolina. It works in San Diego. It works in Seattle, Washington, New York City, and in Miami. I talk to these lawyers all the time, and I know what works.

In this marketing system, follow-up is the holy grail of conversions. That's really the key to it. Many lawyers send out one letter: "If you need our services, give us a call." That's it. Lawyers are more focused on finding another hot lead and forget about nurturing the leads they have in hand. Leads fall through the cracks because they don't have follow-up systems.

These systems are not complex to put in place. They will take a bit of your time, but the payback is tenfold. Don't market like everyone else. Do what it takes to set yourself apart and be different. Educate, don't sell.

Be Real

You can delegate these processes, the actual tasks. But when it comes to what you're going to do and how you are going to say it—what we call your "voice"—you don't delegate that to anybody. It's got to be from you because it has to be real. It has to reflect you.

I'm a country guy. I come across as a country guy. I'm fine with that. I probably would not do as well in New York City as I do down here, and I understand that. I make sure that my ads do reflect who I am. I use certain words that probably wouldn't be used in San Diego, but it works down here. I don't want somebody in San Diego writing my ads for me.

When they actually come in to meet with you, there has to be that consistency there that okay, that's the guy I saw in the video, he's the same guy.

Just be conversational. When you are filming a video, sit down like you're talking to somebody in your office or in your den. It's all right if you make a few mistakes or blunders, because that's the real world. I mess up sometimes when I am making a video. I smile about it and say, "Hey, I meant to say this."

If you try to be too smooth or sophisticated, the viewers will see through that. Once I was cross-examining a woman in a jury trial. She was so smooth. Usually I was great at making witnesses mad and getting them in my pocket. That was one of my strengths. I could get under their skin in cross-examination, especially if they were lying. But not her. I could not break her. I thought we had lost the case. But we won! The jurors told me that the woman was just too smooth. She wasn't real.

So in your videos, be genuine. That alone will attract enough people to give you the client flow you need.

Do the Math

Think about it this way: if I get 100 leads each month and don't follow up, I may convert 10 of them into cases.

If I set up my system, I will increase my conversion rate to 20 percent. I just doubled my conversion rate, which means I just cut my cost per case in half. I just doubled my profit by doing one thing, by having a follow-up system.

If my average case is $5,000, and I can go from 10 cases to 20 cases, I just made an extra $50,000 a month and an extra $600,000 a year. We're talking about big money. You do that for 10 years, that's $6 million.

If you follow up only a little, and you go from 10 cases to 13 cases, that's an extra $180,000 a year. Somebody says, "Well, it won't increase this much if I don't get one hundred leads or whatever."

Whatever you do, whatever percentage you increase it by, it's going to be more money in your pocket, because you aren't spending more money on advertising. Your system is working for you.

The people who sell media advertising always talk about reach and frequency; how many people you will reach and how often you are going to reach them. Transfer that equation to this system.

A prospect opts into your system. You've now reached them. And you will continue to reach out to them. It's a reach and frequency you control because you built the system. And you're your media, not the ones being sold by the media reps. Having your own media and your own system is smart marketing.

Studies have shown that 80 percent of consumers who need to hire a doctor, dentist, or lawyer don't choose one until they have made five to seven inquiries.

So how many times do you reach out to a prospect? To maximize your chances, based on the studies of consumer behavior, you had better reach out at least seven times. I have reached out

26 times in six months to some prospects in my system. It's all automated and purposeful.

Some people will try to represent themselves on Social Security cases, and they lose the first battle (which might take up to four to five months) before they realize they need a lawyer. After all that time, all of the other lawyers, even the smart lawyers who are doing what I'm doing, are giving up. Not me. I'm still contacting them. The prospect thinks, "They called me. They know my name. They're still here. I like them. I think I'll call them." It's all about top-of-mind awareness. Stay on the top of their minds long after your competition stopped contacting them.

When I first started, I had my staff just keep a list of everybody, where they heard about us, what their problems were, and their names and addresses. Now, this was back in the mid-1980s, before we had computers. We did it by hand and on simple spreadsheets. Most importantly, I wanted to know where each prospect came from.

Create these reports, regardless of what software or system you use, so you'll know where your prospects are coming from. Educate, build trust, and get people to know and like you. Then you want to track these conversions. How many of these people actually end up hiring you? Those are some of the numbers you need to know if your sales machine is going to generate more business for you year after year.

Not only have reports come a long way, but I have also changed the way I measure conversions. Say 200 people call me in a month. Of those 200, there might be only 60 people that I really want. The other 140 I really don't want for any number of reasons. Of those 60 that I want, maybe I get 40. So out of 200 leads, I converted 40, which would be a conversion rate of 20 percent.

But that is not a good measure. The important number is how many of the 60 desirable prospects did I convert? What I really want to know is out of those 60 that I wanted, how many of those did I really convert? If I'm only converting 40 out of 60, then I'm not doing a very good job, because I should be converting 90 percent.

Sometimes the question you ask is not the right question. Now I ask myself: How many conversions am I getting from the leads that I really want? My staff knows I want 100 percent, but I can live with 95 percent.

It carries over into other aspects of our business. A lot of lawyers ask me: "What percentage of my gross revenue should I spend for marketing?"

My answer is: "That is the wrong question, my friend. The question is, 'How many cases do you want next year?'"

"I want all I can get."

"No," I say. "How many cases can you afford? Do you know what your average fee is?"

"Yeah."

"Do you know what your cost per case is for your different types of marketing?"

"Well, yeah."

"Well then, tell me how much you want to grow. If you know an average case costs you $300, and you're spending $10,000 a month now and getting 30 cases, if you want 60 cases, I'll tell you you're going to spend $20,000. Wrong question."

The right question is, "How much am I spending per case in each medium?"

The legendary businessman John Wanamaker once said, "Half the money I spend on advertising is wasted; the trouble is I don't know which half." To put it into our context, you could restate it: I know 50 percent of my marketing works, I just don't know which 50 percent. Today is different. With technology and by asking the right questions, we can know where 80 or 90 percent of your business is coming from.

Lawyers ask: "Who told you about me?"

I used to ask the same thing, but that's not enough anymore. Now I ask: "What did you look at when you dialed my number?"

Maybe they had seen me on TV or a neighbor had given them a copy of the newsletter with my telephone number on it.

If you've set up your machine properly, you've built an integrated marketing and sales machine that all works together. Knowing the answers to these questions helps you keep your machine finely tuned.

I have this philosophical debate with lawyers all the time, and with some marketing people. They say there's no way, if you're doing a lot of things, if you've got a big budget, there's no way to know exactly where your business is coming from. And they're right, to a certain degree. I'd rather know when I can, though. Every bit of information that I can get is going to be important to me with regards to my decisions.

It's part of the whole marketing system. You can have as archaic a system as I had when I started my practice, or you can have a more sophisticated system like Infusionsoft or Needles, which is my case management software. It can actually tell me how many leads and conversions we get each day or week or month or year or whatever. I can set the dates up, it will tell me how many new intakes, which means leads that I got, or prospects, depending on your definition. How many are pending and how many rejected us? I can sit there any time and pull up a report, (looking back in time or live data) instantaneously of what's going on with my marketing.

Prior to all the technology that is available today, we used to do it the old-fashioned way, which is still better than not doing it at all. Fortunately, most lawyers aren't doing this at all, which gives me (and you) a big advantage.

Chapter 4

Sales Machine Marketing Tactics

Important Numbers

In setting up your sales machine, you need to know what I call the three big numbers.

1. Your Average Fee

2. Your Average Cost Per Lead

3. Your Average Cost Per Case

Average Fee

In order to figure the return on my investment, I need to know my average fee. For instance, if I am a domestic lawyer whose average fee is $5,000, then I know that I can probably spend $800 to get a case. I really don't want to, but I know that I can. I'd prefer to spend $300 per case.

Average Cost Per Lead

But how do I know how much I can spend to get a case if I don't know my cost per lead or my conversion rate? Let's start with cost per lead.

If I get 100 leads, and I know that those hundred leads cost me $3,000, then that's $30 per lead. What if my cost were $30,000 for 100 leads? Then my cost per lead would be $300.00.

Average Cost Per Case

Cost per case is found by combining your cost per lead with your conversion percentage. Personally, I know that I convert 10% of my leads to clients. Continuing the previous example, if I spend $3,000 for 100 leads and convert 10% of those leads, I'm getting 10 cases. That means my cost per case is $300.

With my fee of $5,000 per case, I make $50,000 off of my initial $3,000 spend. That's a 16-to-1 ROI. Once I know that, I can make adjustments and tweak my costs.

But what if I had to spend $30,000 for those 100 leads instead of $3,000? Then my cost per case is $3,000. I'm only getting an ROI of 1.6, which is bad—very bad.

When I started doing TV in 1998, my cost per case was about $300 to $400. Now it's $1,200. I no longer do regular 30-second commercial spots for Social Security on regular TV because my cost is too much. I'm doing infomercials, which are a better return. I've got to keep my cost per case at $300.

I also use the Internet. I'm getting cases from the Internet at less than $200 per case. How do I know this? I track it. You must know your numbers and measure everything. That is part of your marketing sales machine.

Ken Hardison's Easy ROI Calculator

Here's an easy ROI calculator you can use to monitor the effectiveness of your marketing campaigns. You need to know four things about a campaign to use this calculator:

- Average Fee
- Total Campaign Cost
- Number of Leads Gained
- Number of Cases Gained

You should be able to obtain all of those without much difficulty. You know your average fee, you had better know the cost of the campaign, and you can easily track the number of leads and cases gained.

After we go through the calculator step-by-step, I will plug the examples we just used into it so you can see the calculator in action.

STEP 1

	_____	(Total Campaign Cost)
÷	_____	(Number of Leads Gained)
=	_____	(Average Cost Per Lead)

STEP 2

	_____	(Number of Cases Gained)
÷	_____	(Number of Leads Gained)
=	_____	(Lead Conversion Percentage)

STEP 3

      _____ (Lead Conversion Percentage)

x   _____ (Average Cost Per Lead)

=   _____ (Average Cost Per Case)

STEP 4

      _____ (Number of Cases Gained)

x   _____ (Average Fee)

=   _____ (Total Fees)

STEP 5

      _____ (Number of Cases Gained)

x   _____ (Average Cost Per Case)

=   _____ (Total Costs)

STEP 6

      _____ (Total Fees)

÷   _____ (Total Costs)

=   _____ (Return on Investment)

Not too complicated, is it? Let's try it with the two earlier examples.

Example 1

- Average Fee = $5,000
- Total Campaign Cost = $3,000
- Number of Leads Gained = 100
- Number of Cases Gained = 10

STEP 1

	_____3,000_____	(Total Campaign Cost)
÷	_____100_____	(Number of Leads Gained)
=	_____30_____	(Average Cost Per Lead)

STEP 2

	_____10_____	(Number of Cases Gained)
÷	_____100_____	(Number of Leads Gained)
=	_____10_____	(Lead Conversion Percentage)

STEP 3

	_____10_____	(Lead Conversion Percentage)
x	_____30_____	(Average Cost Per Lead)
=	_____300_____	(Average Cost Per Case)

STEP 4

	_____10_____	(Number of Cases Gained)
x	_____5,000_____	(Average Fee)
=	_____50,000_____	(Total Fees)

STEP 5

	_____10_____	(Number of Cases Gained)
x	_____300_____	(Average Cost Per Case)
=	_____3,000_____	(Total Costs)

STEP 6

	_____50,000_____	(Total Fees)
÷	_____3,000_____	(Total Costs)
=	_____16.7_____	(Return on Investment)

So this campaign produced a 16.7 ROI. The lawyer received $16.70 in return for every $1.00 spent! That's a successful campaign by my reckoning.

Example 2

Notice that only the Total Campaign Cost changes. But when it does, the ROI is dramatically affected!

- Average Fee = $5,000
- Total Campaign Cost = $30,000
- Number of Leads Gained = 100
- Number of Cases Gained = 10

STEP 1

	_____30,000_____	(Total Campaign Cost)
÷	_____100_____	(Number of Leads Gained)
=	_____300_____	(Average Cost Per Lead)

STEP 2

	_____10_____	(Number of Cases Gained)
÷	_____100_____	(Number of Leads Gained)
=	_____10_____	(Lead Conversion Percentage)

STEP 3

	_____10_____	(Lead Conversion Percentage)
x	_____300_____	(Average Cost Per Lead)
=	_____3,000_____	(Average Cost Per Case)

STEP 4

	_____10_____	(Number of Cases Gained)
x	_____5,000_____	(Average Fee)
=	_____50,000_____	(Total Fees)

STEP 5

	_____10_____	(Number of Cases Gained)
x	_____3,000_____	(Average Cost Per Case)
=	_____30,000_____	(Total Costs)

STEP 6

	_____50,000_____	(Total Fees)
÷	_____30,000_____	(Total Costs)
=	_____1.67_____	(Return on Investment)

This campaign was a lot less successful. The ROI was 1.67, which means that the lawyer only got $1.67 for every $1.00 spent.

I have a rule of thumb for my return on investment: If I can't get six times my money back in a particular campaign, I either have to tweak my marketing or get out of it. I want 10 or 15 times my money back, but six is my threshold. I'll tweak it for about 90 days. After that, if I can't get my ROI up to six times or better, then I'm dumping the campaign and putting my money somewhere else.

You have to determine your personal ROI threshold, whether that be three or six or ten times your investment. I think this ROI calculator will help you to do just that.

This is a short chapter, but the message is huge. In setting up your sales machine, you need to know your three big numbers.

1. Average Fee
2. Average Cost Per Lead
3. Average Cost Per Case

Knowing, monitoring, and building systems to leverage these big three numbers will pay massive dividends for years to come. These systems are an integral part of your sales marketing machine, a machine that you have to maintain in order to receive an optimized rate of return.

Chapter 5

Sales Machine Marketing Tactics —Before Representation

In creating this sales machine, you've got to attract people, track your traffic, capture the information, nurture them, and convert them. You will need different marketing tactics to feed your machine. There are online and offline tactics.

When I plan my marketing strategy, I think about what people do immediately before and after the event that has required them to hire a lawyer. In a car wreck, for instance, a person may go to the hospital, a doctor a chiropractor. They may talk to an insurance agent or take their car to a body shop.

A person in a divorce usually sees a pastor or a counselor before the divorce and often afterwards. Sometimes they try a dating service. They almost always see a lawyer.

If you have a book, your book could be in that doctor's office lobby as they are sitting there. What better place to pick up one of your books?

The point here is for you to think about what your prospects are doing before they contact a lawyer. Put your message there, and you'll attract a lot more leads.

Websites

The most important thing on your website is an opt-in option that allows a prospect to ask for something, such as a free report. In return, you get contact information about the prospect.

A lot of the websites have the name of the firm big and up high. At my website, Carolina SSD Lawyers, the name of my firm is up there, but it's very small. The big headline on my website is: "How to Double Your Chances of Winning Your Social Security Case."

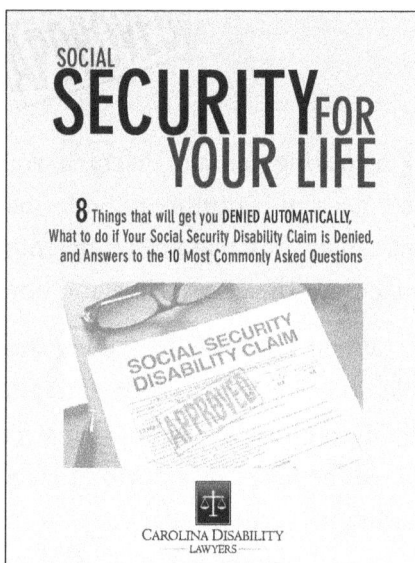

SOCIAL
SECURITYFOR
YOUR LIFE

8 Things that will get you DENIED AUTOMATICALLY,
What to do if Your Social Security Disability Claim is Denied,
and Answers to the 10 Most Commonly Asked Questions

SOCIAL SECURITY
DISABILITY CLAIM

APPROVED

CAROLINA DISABILITY
LAWYERS

One of the free reports we offer online

It's got nothing to do with me. I'm the solution, but I'm trying to get them to stay on my website. To do that, I need a lot more than a pretty picture of me with Carolina Disability Lawyers in the logo. Everybody does that. I want to differentiate myself.

I want to have live chat on my website and strong calls to action: "Download this free report." "Watch my video."

Give visitors multiple ways to engage with you—your bounce rate will go down and your conversion rate will go up.

Pay-Per-Click

Pay-per-click (PPC) is nothing more than buying ads on Google or Bing or Yahoo or some other online search engine. When someone clicks on your ad, then you pay a fee. PPC can be a very effective way to attract leads. After clicking on your ad, you want them to go to a landing page tailored for that specific ad instead of to your website.

You should have a great call to action just like you do on your website. Headlines are very important. In order to entice someone to click your ad, you need to spark their curiosity or hit what we'll call a trigger. Emotional triggers are things that make people take action.

I've found a couple of triggers that really work for my firm. One is an appeal to people's greed, especially for personal injury lawyers. The other one is fear of loss, like domestic criminal lawyers. Fear of losing my driver's license. Fear of losing the right to see my kids. Fear of losing my property because my wife's going to take it all.

You need to hit those emotional triggers on pay-per-click ads. Entice a prospect to your landing page, and then give him the headline that will cause him to take an action that will allow you to capture his information. Then you can nurture this lead and convert him into a paying client.

Autoresponders

Once they opt-in, your autoresponder email system goes into gear. There are different companies offering autoresponder technology at a variety of price ranges. Choose one that fits your needs. You can choose from iContact, Infusionsoft, MailChimp, or one of the others out there.

Remarketing

Remarketing is the feature that drops "cookies" onto a prospect's computer when he visits your website. Then, as he continues searching, even though he might bounce off your page, your ad will keep popping up most everywhere he goes. The key to it is you don't have to pay for all of these impressions unless he actually clicks on the ad.

Your remarketing ad can offer something different than your PPC ad does, such as a free report. You can catch a lead with a headline such as: "The 3 Things You Should Never Tell Your Spouse When You're Getting Ready to Leave." When they see that, they'll click to get your free report and your sales machine is off to the races. Remarketing is very cost effective.

Remarketing also makes you look bigger than you are because they see your ad everywhere they go. It's really very cool technology that you should be using.

YouTube

You can put your videos on YouTube, but I prefer private hosting so that my competition's videos don't pop up when a prospect has looked at mine. I like to use something like Vimeo, which you can use for only $200 or $300 per year. It's all a matter of controlling the environment in which they see my ad.

If you don't want to use a private service, then by all means, use YouTube. Just be sure you have video as part of your marketing sales machine.

Blogs

Blogs are another important part of your sales machine, and they can be very helpful for SEO (Search Engine Optimization). Blogs give your prospects more opportunity to learn about you, and if you do it right, your blog is fresh and current. At the end of the blog, you can offer a free report for download.

Blogs don't have to be short or long, but they do need to be informative. You can even do a video blog (Vlog) using your smart phone. Upload that to YouTube and your website and you are good to go.

Remember, you are providing educational information here. You are not selling. You always want to offer them more information through your free report, etc., but you never want to come across as a salesperson. Remember, the more you tell, the more you sell.

Infographics

Some people don't like to read, but they love to look at pictures, and an infographic is a great way to do that. I now use infographics for my Social Security marketing.

I have created an infographic about the entire process walking them through it all from applying to appealing to the federal court. It's a great visual way for them to "see" themselves working with our firm.

By explaining the process simply for a prospect, I demonstrate the difficulty of the case and illustrate why they need a lawyer. My hope is that this captures a prospect's attention and keeps him on my website longer.

If prospects are looking at an infographic on my website, and the live chat window pops up, I have an opportunity to engage them. That's the importance of having a lot of these different things working together. It's called a system for a reason, and it's all part of your sales machine.

Facebook

Twitter and Facebook are all the rage right now. To be honest with you, I'm not a big fan of Twitter for law practices. I think it has its place, but I like Facebook better for a number of reasons.

Facebook is like a digital newsletter. I'm trying to keep myself on the top of the minds of clients and prospective clients alike. My posts aren't selling, rather they are informing my followers. I am personalizing myself with posts about my life, such as my hobbies, family activities and happenings. These posts don't have a thing to do with law. Facebook is a *social* media platform.

I write a lot about fishing and golfing, about activities with my kids, and I tell stories about my dog. Also, once in a while, I will write about things going on with the Social Security Administration, the hearings and things like that. But I don't get technical.

I'm giving them information about me, about what's going on with my area of practice. I never write, "If you've been in a wreck, call us." That's more like chasing. That's where lawyers get bad names. That goes against everything I've been saying because our sales machine is not set up that way. Our sales machine is set up to educate, not to chase.

Another thing I like about Facebook is that you can use Facebook ads and enhance them with videos and free reports. You can figure out who your audience is. Facebook Audiences, or Custom Audiences, enables you to see what your demographics are, and do a pay-per-click campaign using Facebook. You can shoot ads out in your geographic area for your demographic.

That is a great marketing strategy, and you don't have to be a genius. If you're a techie, you can do it yourself. I'm not a techie, so I pay people to do this for me. If you can't afford to hire someone, find a high school or college kid in your area. They'll be able to do this for you easily and for a lot less than hiring another employee. You could also check out e-lance.com to find a freelancer who can handle these sorts of projects.

Offline Marketing

Direct Mail

Direct mail is still alive and well. A bankruptcy lawyer can pull a list of people with bad credit scores. If you want motorcycle cases, you can pull the DMV report for everyone in your geographic area who owns a motorcycle. For auto accidents in some states, you can actually pull the accident report as soon as it is filed. Then you direct mail a letter to everyone on the list.

For dog-bite cases, I can go to the local animal control office, because every time someone reports a dog bite, they have to file a report.

Once you start thinking this way, direct mail is still a great way to acquire leads. It's highly targeted and allows you to speak directly to the questions, fears and concerns of your prospect. And when you offer them answers to their questions, they'll like you. The more you tell, the more you sell.

Direct mail doesn't work for all practices. We still send direct mail in Raleigh, my old firm. We get accident reports, but the problem is that someone who has been in a car accident, for instance, will receive mail from 30 different lawyers.

Instead of sending the same old letter—"I see you got in a wreck. We're here for you. Get a free case review."—we send them reports with information such as "11 Questions You Should Ask the Insurance Adjuster Before You Sign Anything." People are going to read that. We are using great headlines. We are hitting their emotional triggers.

I've actually had people call me and say, "You know, I got all of these letters from all of these lawyers, but man, this report you had about what the adjuster was going to do to me, it's like you're a mind reader and you knew exactly what was going to happen. So I want to hire you. You know what you're doing."

Direct mail is a more targeted approach, and you get a better return on your investment. We have the whole system set up to mail multiple pieces. It was all designed to provide them with more and more information. In North Carolina, we can use testimonials, so we put in our testimonials, we put in our verdicts, and not to brag about ourselves, but this shows they can trust us to handle their case. Especially if their emotional trigger is greed, they're wanting the most money they can get.

Television

Television is very expensive. It's not for everyone. If you can't be in the top three or four in your market, I say don't do it. It's a mass media, but you can do direct response television ads—that's what I like about it. You can do different types of commercials, but the problem is that now the medium is cluttered. Twenty years ago, there were three TV stations. Now, with cable, there are 500 outlets, and everybody's doing Netflix and streaming. It's not as effective as it once was. It's still very effective, but it's a big play, and most lawyers just can't afford it. If you want to do TV advertising at a discounted rate, there is a company called Wholesale Airtime Auction (www.WholesaleAirtimeAuction.com) that I would highly recommend. Tell them I sent you—I've been using them for over 5 years.

Radio

Radio is good for hitting a certain demographic, because stations cater to different tastes in music and news. The two best things for a lawyer is to either host your own talk show or hook up with one of the radio celebrities. Have one endorse you on his morning talk show, become sort of a co-celebrity, and ride on his or her coattails. Become the local expert.

These two options are better because they give listeners a chance to get to know you. As they do, they'll come to like you and trust you. Then, when they have a need, they'll call you.

Don't look for immediate results, though. Radio is a long-distance runner in the media world. Be consistent, provide information, and position yourself as the expert who is approachable. When you do this, radio can be a very good addition to your marketing sales machine.

Festivals

We do a number of festivals and flea markets. We set up our booths, hand out our books and our reports, and answer questions. We usually give away a big prize. We'll take a TV and a

DVD player and run videos the entire time, and then we'll have a drawing for the TV. To enter, they must put their name, address and email address on the drawing slip, then we draw a name and give it away. We all win. We don't have to take the TV back, and we capture a big list of people to add to our newsletter list.

Billboards

Billboards are not a good medium unless you're doing TV or radio because the primary purpose of billboards is to be a reminder and reinforce TV and radio commercials. I have not met a lawyer who could tell me his ROI for billboards unless he was already doing heavy TV or radio advertising.

Books and Reports

My favorites, of course, are books and reports, because those are the foundation of my education-based marketing theory—that the more you educate, the more they are going to trust you.

We know from the Alyn-Weiss report mentioned earlier that approachability and trustworthiness are two big issues when someone is picking a lawyer. I think having your own book and offering free reports reinforces that position. It goes back to my adage that people hire lawyers they like and trust. That's one reason I've written so many books. I want people to see me as the expert in my field and the person they can trust to solve their problems.

Newsletters

A newsletter is good because it is another way to remind people that you are available, and a newsletter allows you to position yourself in their memory. Top of Mind Awareness (TOMA) is important because, as I've said previously, not everyone is going to hire you this week. By sending them your newsletter you will be there when they need you. It's also an easy way for them to tell a friend or neighbor about you. Having your own print newsletter is one of the first steps in setting up your marketing sales machine.

Press Releases

Generally, I use a press release for linking to my website, but a press release can be most effective when you are linking to a news event. I'll send out one in which I make a controversial statement so that I grab the attention of the local newspaper or the news stations. When reporters call you for an interview on a current event, they give you instant credibility.

When Merck recalled Vioxx in 2004, I was in Vegas at a Mass Torts conference, and I had written a press release that said I was out there. A reporter for the *Raleigh News & Observer*, the biggest newspaper in Raleigh, called me for an interview. I was in Vegas learning all about it, so she quoted me with four or five sentences from our conversation. I picked up about 20 Vioxx cases from that one press release and interview.

Vioxx was in the news. It was the conversation on everybody's mind. It was a hot topic, so I rode the wave. You can use PR Web, or PR Wire news, and they will float your press release out to many media outlets for you. It's all pretty simple. Just takes a bit of thinking and a little action.

You can stay abreast of likely issues with web alerts. A domestic lawyer can use Google Alerts to alert him every time something is in the news about domestic law.

To keep up with DWI, you can set up several Google alerts such as: DWI North Carolina; DWI convictions North Carolina; North Carolina Law on DWIs. Google will send you or a staff member a notice whenever that phrase is found. Stay on top of what's happening in the news.

I use Google Alerts for legal marketing. Anytime something comes up about legal marketing or lawyer advertising, Google sends me an email. I want be alert to what's going on. Google Alerts is a good (and free) way to do this.

Print Ads

For print ads, just follow these rules for headlines and the body copy:

1. Agitate

2. Propose a solution

3. Offer a good call to action

You can learn more about writing print ads in Chapter 2.

Chapter 6

Sales Machine Marketing Tactics —During Representation

Client Service

A referral is much less expensive than any kind of media you can buy, and you don't have to go through all of the nurturing because somebody has already done that for you. Others will refer a client to you because they know you provide a good service. Referral cases are also normally better cases because people who like you won't refer a bad case to you.

You need to have systems built to generate referrals from your happy clients. These can be surveys, emails, events, or one of my favorites—send clients a signed copy of my book with two or three extras for them to hand out. Doing this immediately after you win their case is the ideal time since that's when they are going to be talking about you and how great you are.

It's easy for them to hand a copy of my book to someone as they say, "This is the guy who won my case. He's the best!" This is how you teach your clients and friends to refer you cases. It takes the heavy lifting off of them.

Then their friend reads my book, gets to know, like, and trust me and we're on the road to another client.

Create Raving Fans

You want to create raving fans, and just giving great client service is not enough anymore. You must give exceptional service and WOW! people. As Walt Disney said, you want to give them something to talk about. You want to create such an atmosphere that they can't help but talk about you. To do that, you must offer things that no other firm offers.

Every firm ought to have a mission statement that explains its core values and vision. You want to attract employees who share your core values, who understand that if not for the clients, there would be no paycheck. The clients are the easiest mini-marketers you can get. These people have problems, or they wouldn't be there. And if not for the grace of God, you could be in their shoes, whether it be a DWI, a divorce, a car wreck, a will contest or a land condemnation.

Everyone has a problem. Our job is to care for them as we help them find a solution. To do that consistently, we have created, as part of our marketing sales machine, a client service manual.

This manual has developed over time. It lists our mission statement, core values, corporate responsibilities, and client expectations. It is a living document that continues to evolve. It's also one that every new employee reads and adheres to. It's a must if we are going to provide exceptional customer service.

Client Loyalty Mentality

The Doctrine of Preeminence

The best way to create client loyalty is to adhere to what Jay Abraham calls the Doctrine of Preeminence: Everything you do is for the betterment of your clients. You put them first, from opening the file to closing the file and everything in between. You want to become their trusted legal advisor. It's all about trust.

Now that our machine has created the trust, we want to create client loyalty and raving fans. The benefit, of course, is referrals and repeat business.

Some lawyers say, "I only do one kind of law, and I don't want people asking me questions about other stuff."

They're missing the boat. I want prospects calling me every time they've got a problem, because I don't want them just to guess whether or not I handle a particular kind of case. I don't want another Joe walking into a courtroom with a cast on his leg with a lawyer other than me handling his case. Even if I wasn't handling personal injury, if I was his trusted legal advisor, he would have called me and I would have referred him to someone that I trust. I would have gotten a referral fee and Joe would get a great lawyer.

If a case doesn't pay a referral fee, then we go to the Doctrine of Reciprocity. When I refer a prospect to a lawyer, I send him a note saying, "I referred you John Doe. I hope you'll take care of him." When you alert a lawyer that you have done this, he will send cases back to you. Most lawyers want to reciprocate. Not every lawyer does, but more than 50 percent of them will.

The Grandma Test

Another way to create client loyalty is the Grandma Test, which I stole from Jeffrey Gitomer, a sales and marketing consultant guru. I tell members of my staff to talk to a client as if they were talking to their grandma. When you're on the phone with a client, put Grandma at the end of a sentence. Would you say to your Grandma, "I'm going to put you on hold for a couple of minutes, Grandma?" No, you wouldn't. Use the Grandma Test to improve your client relations on the phone, and in person.

Another thing we do is Celebrate a Client. If we learn that something good has happened to a client—their child got an award or a baby was recently christened—we send a card. My receptionist writes the card, and I sign it. It's handwritten.

It's going that extra step, creating that relationship and trust and that bond so that when they leave you, and you close out the case, even if the case didn't come out the way they wanted it to, they remember you and like you. They will refer people to you. Why? Because people refer to lawyers they know, like, and trust.

One way I personalize myself is to say folksy things a client will remember. I am sort of folksy, and so when I say these things, it is authentic. In North Carolina, when we didn't have legalized gambling, I told everybody that we actually did have legalized gambling – It's called the jury system, because there's two things in the world you never know: What a little boy's got in his pocket and what a jury's going to do. Sometimes a case goes bad even when you have done your best.

You just never know.

If they are confident you are doing the best you can, if you treat them with respect and you care about them, and you're their trusted legal advisor, they are going to refer people to you. Even if you lose the case.

Client Loyalty Secrets

A little while ago I wrote an article titled "10 Secrets to Developing Client Loyalty." Since this section of the book is about client loyalty, I thought I would reproduce the article here in its entirety. These ten simple yet powerful tips will turn anyone who implements them into a client loyalty pro!

10 Secrets to Developing Client Loyalty

Potential clients are bombarded by over 3,000 messages a day meant to persuade their spending habits. Whether it's the billboard they drive past every day to work, the label on the bottle of Pepsi they're drinking, or the Cadillac emblem on the car they're stuck behind in traffic, these visual messages are meant to create top-of-mind-awareness and persuade the consumer the next time they're in the market to buy a certain product or service. With the huge number of messages that reach them every day, it's no wonder that consumer habits can change at the drop of a hat.

Client loyalty is of the utmost importance. Simplistic messages that create top-of-mind-awareness cannot sway the loyal client. While the competition is spending dollars upon dollars on ways to increase client volume, many of them are forgetting the importance of their existing clients. Forgetting this will almost certainly lead to a number of unsatisfied clients, which will likely never become loyal clients.

A loyal client and a satisfied client are not to be confused. While client satisfaction is an element of loyalty, a client could be satisfied and still feel no connection to you or your firm. A loyal client will have these five characteristics:

1. The overall satisfaction of doing business with your law firm.

2. The willingness to build a relationship with you and your company.

3. The willingness to be a repeat client.

4. The willingness to recommend you to others.

5. The reluctance to switch to another law firm.

In order for you to achieve those five things with your clients, there are 10 rules that you and your employees should follow every day:

1. GREET CLIENTS PROMPTLY

A survey clocked the number of seconds people had to wait to be greeted in several businesses. Researchers then asked clients how long they had been waiting. In every case, the client's estimate of the time elapsed was much longer than the actual time. A client waiting 30 or 40 seconds often feels like it's been 3 or 4 minutes. Time drags when people are waiting. Thus, one of the things we can do to greet clients properly is not to put them on hold and to answer the phone on its first ring when being paged by the receptionist.

This is a good time to tell you that one of your best investments is a good receptionist. This person can make or break your firm depending on how well they deal with people. Give this person great latitude to get the call answered, and if the rest of the firm doesn't fall in line, afford this person an open door policy. I have found time and time again that the receptionist knows if you are meeting client satisfaction goals.

2. APPLY GOOD CONVERSATION SKILLS

It is always nice to talk to people like they are in your living room. People in general are intimated by lawyers in law offices. It should be your job to make them feel comfortable, as they have already been through a traumatic event. Something to break the ice would be the weather; for example, "Isn't the sunshine just beautiful?" or "The snowfall's great, isn't it?" Look for clues about the client's interest. Also, you must understand that interaction means that both parties must have an opportunity to participate. If one party monopolizes the conversation, both sides lose.

Some preferred topics are what we refer to as small talk. Americans prefer to talk about weather, sports, jobs, mutual acquaintances, and past experiences, especially ones they have in common with their conversation partners. Most Americans are taught to avoid discussing politics or religion, especially with people they do not know well. Sex, bodily functions, and emotional problems, considered very personal topics, are likely to be discussed only with close friends or professionals trained to help.

3. BUILD A RAPPORT WITH THE CLIENT

Remember that you are building a relationship with your clients. They must know that their case is the top priority, and that you are there for them.

1. Be a good listener

2. Relate to what they are going through

3. Invite feedback

4. BE SINCERE AND SHOW EMPATHY TO THE OTHER PERSON

I have preached for years that *There, but for the grace of God, go I.* You should understand that these people are hurting and coming to us for assistance.

5. USE GOOD PHONE TECHNIQUES

A key to successful phone use is simply to remember that your client cannot see you. Your challenge is to use your voice to make up for all the lost nonverbal communication. The best ways to use the phone effectively are:

1. Give the caller your name. Let the caller know who you are just as you would in a face-to-face situation.

2. Smile into the phone. Somehow people can hear us smile over the phone! Some telephone pros place a mirror in front of them while they are on the phone.

3. Keep your caller informed. If you need to look up information, tell the client what you are doing. Don't leave them holding a dead phone with no clue as to whether you are still with them.

4. Invite the caller to get to the point. Use questions such as "How can I assist you today?" or "What can I do for you?".

5. Commit to the requests of the caller; tell the caller specifically what you will do and when you will get back to them.

6. Thank the caller. This lets the caller know when the conservation is over.

7. Let your voice fluctuate in tone, rate, and volume. You hold people's attention by putting a little life into your

voice. Express honest reactions in expressive ways. Let your voice tone be natural and friendly.

8. Use *hold* carefully. People hate to be put on hold. It is necessary to explain why, and break in periodically to assure them they haven't been forgotten. If what you are doing will take longer than a few minutes, ask the caller if you can call them back. Write down your commitment to call them back and do not miss it.

9. Use friendly, common, tactful words. Never accuse the client of anything, and never convey that the request is an imposition.

6. ENJOY PEOPLE AND THEIR DIVERSITY

Every person is different; each has a unique personality. People who tend to bug us the most are the ones who are not like us. Recognize this, then accept this diversity and learn to enjoy it. Know that people's needs are basically the same; similarly, when we treat them like guests, with dignity and courtesy, it will create good will most of the time.

7. CALL PEOPLE BY THEIR NAMES

People love to hear their names. Think about the times when someone unexpectedly addressed you by your name. Didn't you like that? Didn't you feel less like a number and more like someone who is valued?

People appreciate it when you make the effort to learn their name and use it. Here are some ways to make the most of names:

1. When appropriate, introduce yourself to the client and ask his or her name.

2. Avoid being overly familiar too quickly. It's normally safe to address people as Mr. Smith or Mrs. Jones. It could be seen as rude if you call someone by her first name too quickly.

3. If you aren't sure how to pronounce the name, ask the client.

4. If a person has an unusual or interesting name, comment on it in a positive way.

5. If a person shares a name with someone in your family or with a friend, comment on that.

People are usually proud of their names and will feel honored when you acknowledge it. Take time to learn and use your clients' name.

8. WEAR YOUR SMILE WHEN A CLIENT COMES INTO THE OFFICE

Always put on your smile when somebody comes into the office. Be complimentary. Complimenting takes only a second and can build enormous good will. If you don't do this very often, get into the habit of saying something complimentary to each of your clients. Safe grounds for sincere compliments include:

1. An article of their clothing

2. Their children

3. Their behavior

4. Something they own

5. Their helpfulness; for example, "Thank you for filling out the forms so carefully, that will help."

9. FISH FOR NEGATIVE FEEDBACK

What? Fish for negative feedback? Exactly. Negative feedback is the kind that helps you improve. In client service, there is no neutral gear; we either move forward or we slip backward. The best way to get feedback is to let clients know that you really want their honest opinion—good or bad news—and provide ways for them to tell you.

A good way to do this is to use open-ended questions when people express their ideas. An open-ended question cannot be answered with a simple yes, no, or a one-word response. Below are common questions you hear every day in businesses that can be easily changed to open-ended:

Instead of saying:	Say:
"How was everything?"	"What else can I do for you?"
"Can I get you something else?"	"What else can I get for you?"
"Will that be all?"	"What else can I do for you?"
"Was everything satisfactory?"	"What else could we do better to serve you?"
"Did we meet your needs?"	"How else can we be of help?"

10. LIVE BY THE GOLDEN RULE

I have preached this ever since I started practicing law. Simply put, *Treat people the way you would want to be treated.*

These rules are so simple, it constantly amazes me that other law firms do not put them into play. I have come to realize that it's the leadership's responsibility to set the standards. These rules as the basis of a client loyalty program have to be non-negotiable. You absolutely, 100 percent must be willing to terminate your highest income producer or your best non-lawyer, if he doesn't believe in client loyalty. I have done it and never regretted it.

Client Loyalty Practical Tips

There are a few more very practical strategies that you can implement in order to increase your clients' loyalty.

Handwritten Thank-You Notes

When somebody refers a client to our firm, the lawyer who takes the case must send a hand-written thank-you note to the person who made the referral. We found that if you do that, people will keep sending you cases. If you don't, they think you don't care and don't appreciate it, and they aren't going to send you anymore.

I know this from personal experience. I once sent several cases to a doctor. He never acknowledged my referrals. After about three cases, I quit sending people to him, even though he was a good doctor.

It's the Golden Rule. It's so simple, yet so hard, especially for lawyers for some reason.

Mail Stickers

Another strategy in our system is the "We Appreciate Referrals" stickers we put on every piece of mail that leaves our office. We insert little notes that fit into envelopes. In every piece of mail we send out, we include something letting the recipient know that we love referrals.

That's a marketing system.

It's these little things, and you don't do it all overnight. You just put one in at a time, get it rolling and add another one. If you put one simple system in place, then add one system to it each month, at the end of one year you'll have a marketing sales machine with 12 integrated systems working for you. It's not difficult, but it does take some thinking and time.

Use Your Book

One of my all time favorite systems happens at the end of each case.

When I close a case, and my client asks what they can do for me, I say, "Well, here are three books that I've written. When you are talking with people about your case and how everything turned out, would you just hand them a copy of one of my books? Just say, 'These are the lawyers I trusted to represent me.' Thank you!" That will increase referrals.

There is a rule of thumb that 20 percent of your clients will refer someone no matter what you do; 20 percent will never refer someone to you no matter what you do; and 60 percent would refer someone but they don't know how to or don't know that you would like referrals. I'm doing all of the above to ensure they know that I want referrals, that I appreciate them.

My books do my talking for me. They sell me without me having to sell. One of the features in my book is, "The 8 Questions to Ask a Lawyer Before You Hire Them." Every answer points back to me. Ask a lawyer, for instance, whether they have ever had a bar complaint. I've never had a bar complaint. Ask them whether they have tried more than a thousand Social Security cases. Well, I have. You get the point—lead them to where you want them to go. It's a system.

I use questions that will point out the good things about me and set me apart from other lawyers. So I hand a client a book and say, "All you've got to do is give this book to a friend or family member who needs Social Security representation and tell them this is my lawyer." That takes care of that 60 percent who would refer their friends if they knew how to do it.

This goes back to my whole education-based marketing belief. These books are part of my sales

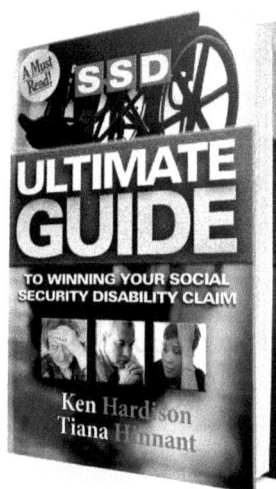

The cover of one of the books we give out

machine. We give them a couple of books when they first become a client. We know they'll be talking with others about their case so that's a great time for them to hand out our books.

What better way to attract new clients than for one of your clients to hand out a book and say, "Here's who we're going with and why. He wrote the book on this." Now you've expanded your sphere of influence and for very little expense.

Having your own book is one of the best ways to attract new leads and generate a flood of referrals. And the best part is you have total control of the message, and it's a system that you can implement for pennies a day.

Chapter 7

Sales Machine Marketing Tactics —After Representation

Top-of-Mind Awareness is Key

This is where a majority of lawyers fail. Everybody understands before representation, and probably 50 percent understand during representation, even if they don't do anything about it.

Ninety percent of lawyers completely blow it when it comes to after representation. They figure the file is closed, I've got the fee, I'm through with this person.

Big mistake!

Why are you going to spend all of that money to attract new leads who don't know you, like you, or trust you when you've got these people with whom you've already built a relationship. Why would you neglect to nurture those people after they leave you? Don't forget about them. That would be a huge waste of money.

The key, like I said about my plumber friend in Myrtle Beach, is to ensure your clients remember you. Most lawyers think, "Well, I represented them, they'll remember me." But people forget. Even when you're representing someone, you might not see him a total of an hour for the whole case. They might remember members of your staff, some of whom probably spend more time with the clients than you do. You need to make them remember you.

Whatever you do, build a system in your After Representation stage. It will become the best system you put in place. Here are some strategies you can use to build this system:

Newsletters

Newsletters are critical to after care. I write mine differently than most lawyers; only 25 percent of my newsletter is about the law, because that's not the purpose of my newsletter. The purpose of my newsletter is to keep me at the front of clients' and prospective clients' minds, to keep developing that relationship. I usually write a lead article about what I'm doing, my vacations, my family. Last year I did a whole series about my daughter's wedding, including a story on how her boyfriend asked her to marry him in a helicopter.

I talk about my fishing trips to Florida, my golfing, and things that are going on at the firm, such as employees' birthdays. We have a recipe of the month, and we normally spotlight a client. For $160 a year, there are services that will provide non-copyrighted tips and copy for your newsletter, everything from safety tips for the winter and Halloween to how to impress your boss. I don't have time to write all of the content, so usually I just write one article myself. We do our newsletter every other month, but every month would be better.

In every newsletter, I write a public thank you to people who have referred cases to me since the last newsletter.

People like to see their names in print. It's another way to reinforce that you appreciate the referrals. I know they read it because one time a woman fell through a crack in our system.

She called me up and said, "Mr. Ken, I referred you so-and-so, and I didn't see my name on your newsletter last month."

"Well I apologize, Miss Lilly," I said. "I tell you what I'm going to do. I'm going to put your name front and center and bold it next time."

In every newsletter, I also tell them, "We want to be your trusted legal advisors. If you have a legal problem, even if it's something we don't handle, call us. We'll get you to a lawyer you can trust and who will handle it competently."

My system includes a list of lawyers for every county surrounding us and their specialties. If somebody calls up, members of my staff don't have to ask me each time. Then, our system requires us to send a note or an email to lawyer Joe Knox saying, "Kathryn so-and-so called today, and we referred her to you. She's got a domestic problem." It's part of the sales machine, because I want to get referrals from other lawyers.

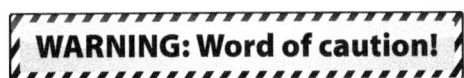

WARNING: Word of caution!

A lawyer called me once and said: "I've been doing this newsletter for six months, and I can't tell if it's doing a thing." You can't give up too quickly!

Give it a full year before you expect to see a marked increase in your referrals. I can't stress this point enough: You can't give up on it too quickly. Also, you've got to be consistent. Send it out on time. Send it out regularly.

A newsletter will work. I know it will. I've been doing it since 1999. To see an example of one of my newsletters, just go to Appendix A.

Birthday Cards

On the Thursday before an upcoming birthday, we prepare cards for our past clients. That job is assigned to my courier. We send out a birthday card that we've had pre-printed. I have my name and my picture, and it says, "Happy Birthday, from Ken." Eighty percent of the people can't tell it's preprinted, 20 percent of the people can, but it doesn't matter. People have called me and said, "I appreciate the card. You're the only person that sent me a birthday card. My own family didn't send me one."

Holiday Cards

Sometimes we send holiday cards. One year for Valentine's Day, we sent a card that said: "We love our clients." We know that no other lawyer in our area did that. We send Thanksgiving Day cards instead of Christmas cards. When we do that, we put in a calendar magnet, because of the plumber. At the bottom of it, we put "We appreciate referrals." These systems all work together.

Client Appreciation Day

Once a year we host a Client Appreciation Day. I'll rent a park and hire a band and face-painting clowns, and rent rides for the children. We have raffles and barbecue, or we cook hot dogs and hamburgers. We might have someone bring a local NASCAR car over and take pictures with kids in front of it. We try to do it in the spring, and a lot of people come. They bring family and friends, and they get to know us. It's just part of building up our approachability factor, that whole deal of trust and relationship. When they leave, we give them a little portable cooler, which includes a magnet, pizza cutter and prescription pill bottle. We also give them a shirt in their particular size. We give them some of our books. It's all part of a system.

I make all the lawyers in my office go to this event. One year I rented a dunking booth, and I made all my lawyers—and myself—spend 30 minutes in that dunking booth. One of the charities we support, Muscular Dystrophy, set up a booth and sold three balls for $3 or so. It gave us a lot of good stuff to write for our newsletter for the next two or three months. And it was for a good cause, and Muscular Dystrophy kept all the money. They didn't raise a lot but it raised awareness. And the fact is, if we were going to get dunked, we wanted somebody to get something out of it other than us getting wet.

Client Advisory Panel

A Client Advisory Panel is an inexpensive way to stay in touch with clients and to make them a part of our process by listening to their thoughts about their experiences.

About three times a year, we'll rent a room at Golden Corral or Ryan's Steakhouse, and buy them all a steak dinner. We give them four questions to answer, such as: "How are we doing?" "What are you hearing about us in the community?" "Any complaints from your friends or family?" "Anything you think we should be doing better?" They feel appreciated, and they send us referrals.

We usually give them a promotional item, something special instead of the junk everybody gives, a promo that costs $20, $25—a clock or a nice Mag flashlight.

Then all my lawyers and I sit around at different tables, and I go around and talk to everybody. I don't even eat. I just go around and talk, see how everybody's doing, how their family's doing, just creating relationships.

If a client thinks that something is wrong, I want to know about it because I can't fix it if I don't know it. We're not perfect. We do make mistakes. So it's a good time for us because they'll tell us. They want us to succeed because they love us.

Again, 90 percent of the lawyers don't do these things that we're doing after we close a client's file. All of this stuff can be systematized. You just set it up on your calendar. We send form letters to clients to ask them to be on the advisory panel.

Then we send out postcards inviting them to the Golden Corral with directions on the back. We also have a note that instructs them to call our receptionist if they have any questions or problems.

Chapter 8

Conclusion

You need a system. But don't expect to build it in a day. Start with one simple system and build from there. Do the little things that no one else is willing to do. Take the time now and make the investment that will pay dividends for years to come.

Maybe start with a simple newsletter. Then add Thank You cards. Next add Birthday cards. Then create an automated follow-up system. Set up your infrastructure so when your processes start to work, you can handle the increase.

Monitor the numbers we've discussed. Split test your ads and landing pages. Remarket your PPC ads. Implement the Grandma Test. And offer a free report or, better yet, write your own book.

Lawyers who follow my advice will increase their business. Our PILMMA members are consistently applying what you have learned here and their firms are growing. You can go to my website at www.PILMMA.org and read their testimonials and watch the videos. These guys are doubling and tripling their practices. It takes them a couple of years to do it. But remember, Rome wasn't built in a day. If you'll follow the advice I've given and build one system every month and stay with it, it will work, and you will be rewarded for it; you and your family.

You can build the practice you've dreamed of, and have the life you've dreamed of. More time with your family, less stress at work, more joy from serving your clients with excellence, and gaining more referrals than you ever thought possible. It's all possible, but it does require action.

Now is the time to act. Set up one system in the next 30 days in each one of these stages:

- Before Representation
- During Representation
- After Representation

Once you begin to see the results, you'll keep doing it. But if you just close this book and put it on the shelf, you're not going to do anything and your time here will have been wasted.

As Robert Ringer says, "Nothing happens until you take action." That's the key. It's like the Nike motto, "Just do it." Take baby steps. The system has elements you can create without spending a lot of money. Think through each stage, determine one—just one—system you will create and do something in the next 24 hours to make that system a reality.

Some parts of your system will require an investment of time, others of money, but most can be created quite easily and for very little money.

Take the first bite of your elephant and get one system up and running in each stage in the next 30 days. Then let me know how it's working for you.

Tap into one of my systems to communicate with me. You no doubt will have ideas I didn't think of. I will be happy to share those in future publications and on my website. Or you can write your own book, just like I have.

Your Next Step

First, let me congratulate you for coming this far. You are one of the 5 percent who will do something with this wealth of knowledge. Few lawyers have the true passion and desire to take the necessary steps to do what it takes to be successful.

This book is only one step to turning your practice into a "sales machine." If you allow me, I will help you in the process of attaining the practice of your dreams. You see, getting cases is only half the battle. You have to hire, train, and motivate your staff and attorneys to handle your increased volume of cases. Below is my offer to you.

Sign up and receive a digital download of the "A-Z Law Practice Management Blueprint" Workshop ($597.00 value). This one-day event completely sold out and is chock-full of forms and processes to effectively hire and manage your staff. Below are just a few of the topics covered:

- Step-by-Step Checklist for New Hires
- Creating Job Descriptions
- Creating an Employee Handbook
- Establishing Benchmarks
- How to Create and Utilize an Onboard Training Manual
- Productivity Tracking
- Motivation Techniques
- Keeping Employee Morale High
- Creating an Organizational Chart
- How to Create a Mission Statement
- How to Interview Applicants Without Getting Fooled

- How to Deal with Toxic and Problem Employees
- How to Create a Salary Structure for Staff that will Motivate Them to Excel
- How to Properly Fire an Employee

Just go to www.LawPracticeAdvisor.com/FreeGift22 and commit to three months of membership in LawPracticeAdvisor.com for only $37.97 per month. Do yourself a favor and get this invaluable information to boost your income and short-cut your road to success.

This is just the beginning of what we will do for you. My entire team is at your disposal. We are here if you are ready. The rest lies in your hands. You can start building a life of true financial freedom today. All you need to do is officially declare your commitment and then follow our programs.

Appendix A

These next four pages are from an actual newsletter that I mailed out in January 2015. I think you'll notice that it is very different from most legal newsletters. I'm trying to build relationships, not just inform. After reading my newsletter, think about how you can change your own newsletter in order to make it more personal and relational—or start your newsletter for the first time! Either way, sending a personal newsletter is a great marketing strategy that every lawyer should implement.

Happy New Year 2015!

I hope all of you had a happy holiday season. 2015 is here in full force. Hopefully, you got a chance to eat some black eyed peas and collards on New Year's Day!

As with everyone, I have made my New Year's resolutions. The biggest resolution I made this year is to not travel as much as I did last year. I often get asked to speak to other lawyers on how to manage their practices more efficiently and on how to give and deliver first class client service. In 2014, I logged over one hundred thousand air miles traveling all over the country speaking. My resolution this year is to keep it under twenty thousand miles. Below is a photo of me speaking at a recent seminar in Las Vegas to a group of Social Security Lawyers from around the United States.

I hope you have made some New Year's resolutions that will enhance your health and enjoyment of life. Just remember it takes 21 days to change a habit. So hold the course for three weeks, and you will have it licked!

I hope you enjoy our newsletter. If you have a special request for an article for the next one, don't hesitate to call and let us know. We are here to serve you and want you to think of us as your personal legal advisor. If we can't help you, we will get you to a lawyer who can.

Until next time,

Ken Hardison

Ken Hardison

Inside this Issue:

1-800-600-7535

Carolina Disability Lawyers
802 41st Avenue South
North Myrtle Beach, SC 29582

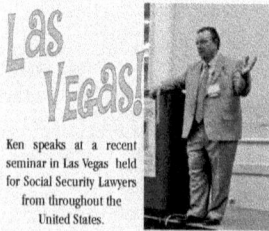

Ken speaks at a recent seminar in Las Vegas held for Social Security Lawyers from throughout the United States.

CAROLINA DISABILITY LAWYERS

MAKE THIS THE YEAR YOUR RESOLUTIONS COME TRUE

Follow these steps to setting good goals and following through...

Is this the year you're really going to achieve your New Year's resolutions? Follow these steps to setting good goals and following through:

• Write down your goals. Make them specific; make sure you can measure the goals. For instance, instead of "Lose some weight," resolve to drop five pounds by June 30.

• Motivate yourself. Write down why you want to achieve the goal. List all the ways you will benefit from achieving it.

• Take stock. Analyze exactly where you are now in reaching that goal. Note the strengths that will help you, the weaknesses that could hurt you, and the opportunities you can use to attain what you want.

• Gather resources. Determine what you'll need to invest to achieve your goal. Whether it's time, money, or something else, know what reaching this goal could "cost" you.

• Commit to learning. You may need to master new abilities to fulfill your resolution. Will you need to take classes to learn a new skill? What kind of information do you need access to?

• Get help. Identify all the people who can serve as your support group. This may also include organizations that can help you.

• Develop a game plan. Set deadlines for achieving your goals. List specific dates on which you want to complete the various steps of the plan.

• Celebrate. Give yourself a reward for achieving the various steps in your game plan and a final reward for achieving the intended goal.

PASS IT ON!

Noteworthy news and information from Carolina Disability Lawyers

Social Security - MySSA

Did you know you could get a ton of information about your claim online? There are a lot of sites out there that may promise you a peek into your claim, but most are unsafe and can't be trusted.

Here's one that can! You can sign up for MySSA accounts at http://www.ssa.gov/myaccount/ and get access to a tremendous amount of information.

Before you receive benefits, you can see:

• Your Social Security statement, with information about annual earnings, estimated Medicare and Social Security taxes paid, work credits earned, and the disability, retirement, and survivors' benefits you and your dependents qualify for.

• A benefit verification letter explaining either that you've never received SSI, SSDI, or Medicare; that you received benefits in the past and they stopped on such and such date; or that your claim for benefits is pending.

Once you start receiving your benefits your MySSA account will allow you to:

• Print a benefits verification letter
• Check earnings records
• Obtain a history of the dates and amounts of benefit payments
• Change addresses and phone numbers
• Start direct deposit or change the account into which your benefits are deposited
• Track the status of requests for reconsideration or waivers if you are contesting an alleged overpayment or other SSA action.

You'll have to give a lot of personal information when signing up for a MySSA account but this is for your protection. They ask for this to verify that you are who you say you are so that no one else can get access to your information. A lot of the questions SSA asks are similar to those used when requesting a credit report. When you open a MySSA account, it will cause a "soft inquiry" on your credit, but this does not change your credit score and does not appear on credit reports. If you don't have a substantial credit history (or if you've recently changed your name), have freezes or fraud alerts on your credit, or don't remember the answers to the questions, you may be unable to enroll online. If you have problems and this happens to you, you must visit an SSA field office to enroll in MySSA. You'll be given a verification code that you can use to complete the sign up process online after you meet with someone at the SSD office to verify that you are who you say you are and you are indeed the one

continued on page 3

Simple Tips For Better Personal Budgeting

"Why is there always so much month left at the end of my money?"

The old joke "Why is there always so much month left at the end of my money?" isn't funny when you're living it all the time. To get control of your finances, you need to approach budgeting rationally and without fear. From the MintLife website come these tips for managing your money successfully:

• **Set a goal.** "Saving money" is not a dream, it's a goal. Before setting out to create a budget, decide precisely what you want: to save $100 a month toward a child's college education, for example, or put away enough money to go on an overseas vacation next year. That gives you something to shoot for.

• **Track your spending.** Whether you do it with a pencil and paper or an iPhone app, record every dollar (or nickel) you spend without fail. If you always forget, you can find secure software that links to your accounts to handle the chore for you automatically.

• **Adjust your time frame.** No law says you have to think in terms of a monthly budget. If that feels too unwieldy, design your budget in weekly or even daily terms so you can monitor your spending and saving more easily.

• **Be honest with yourself.** If you always spend $50 going out to dinner every week, don't pretend you're going to stop next week or the week after. Be realistic. Either include it in your budget, or find some way to offset it somewhere else.

"Every financial worry you want to banish and financial dream you want to achieve comes from taking tiny steps today that put you on a path toward your goals."

Suze Orman

From Your Social Security Lawyer:
Live vs. Video Hearings
Tiana Hinnant, Esq.

In recent months the Social Security Administration has begun trying to schedule more and more Social Security Disability Hearings by VTC: Video Teleconferencing. As you know, the Disability Claim Process often involves 3 distinct stages: the Initial Application, and if denied, then the Reconsideration Phase, and if that is denied, then the Request for Hearing by an Administrative Judge (ALJ). Up until the last few years all Disability Hearings were conducted live at one of the main or satellite Offices of Disability and Review, in areas such as Charleston, Florence, Columbia, Augusta, Myrtle Beach or Wilmington. The main people in the hearing room include the judge, you, your attorney, as well as a Court reporter, and possibly a Vocational Expert. The actual location of your Hearing is determined by where you are residing at the time that your claim is filed or your Hearing is heard. Social Security tries to ensure that your travel distance to the hearing site is less than 75 miles. The actual date, time and place of your hearing will be sent to you by mail in a Notice of Hearing letter.

In what appears to be an attempt on Social Security's part to save travel time and cost, more and more cases are being selected for a possible hearing by video (VTC), with the Judge remaining in his main hearing office, such as Charleston or Columbia, while you and I are in attendance at your nearest satellite office such as Myrtle Beach or Florence. The judge's clerk, who records the proceeding and escorts us into the hearing, is with us at the satellite office. The Vocational Expert may be at either location.

If your case is selected for a possible VTC hearing you will be sent a letter notifying you and giving you the right to agree or object to the video hearing. Many clients call our office when they receive these VTC notification letters, and want my advice on whether or not to agree to a video hearing. Having done many video hearings as well as live hearings, I do NOT usually advise that we object to video hearings unless there is something unusual about a particular case that makes a live hearing necessary. I have found that during the video hearings the judges are able to see and hear us and we are able to see and hear them without any problems. However, if there is something I believe he or she cannot see because it occurs off camera or might not be noticeable, then I will make specific reference to it during the hearing. For example, I might ask that the Record reflect that my client is using a cane, or that she is crying, or perspiring, etc. It has been my experience that Judges appreciate our willingness to accommodate this technology, which allows them to conduct more satellite hearings efficiently.

continued next column

continued from page 2
Social Security - MySSA

trying to open the account.

They are so concerned with your privacy that they forbid third parties from opening MySSA accounts. So basically, you must be the one who opens your account. The MySSA website says:

You cannot create or use an account on behalf of another person, even if you have that person's written permission. You can never share the use of your account with anyone else under any circumstances. Unauthorized use of this service is a misrepresentation of your identity to the federal government and could subject you to criminal or civil penalties, or both.

Given the amount of access a MySSA account provides to your personal and financial information, it is safer for everyone involved, you, your family, your lawyer, if the only person who knows the MySSA account password is you. To protect yourself and your personal information, you should be the only one who can log into the system and show or print information for a representative as needed.

Thank you...
A referral from a former client or friend is the greatest compliment our firm can receive. We are grateful for every referral. Below is a list of people who recently referred a friend or family member to our firm. We would like to publicly thank each and every one of them by listing them in our newsletter. And again, we say, "Thank You!"

Thomas Lasater
Amy S Lawrence, Esq
Patricia Locklear
Lauren Glover
Tiffany Span-Wilder, Esq.
Jim Irvin, Esq.
Rochel Klawsnick

continued from previous column

Please keep in mind that you DO have a right to a face to face hearing with your judge. So you do have every right to object to the VTC hearing if you are uncomfortable with the idea of talking with the judge via video rather than in person. If that is the case, please let our office know when you receive the VTS letter. We will then advise you to sign and return the objection form, so that Social Security knows that you are NOT agreeing to the VTC hearing and wish for them to schedule your hearing at a time and place where the hearing can be live rather than by VTC. I do want to warn you that our objection to the VTC hearing may result in it taking SS a little longer to calendar and hear your case. The choice is yours.

As always we at CDL are committed to helping you win your Social Security case and to do all that is within our power to ensure you obtain an approval as quickly as possible. Thank you for allowing us to help you with your case!

Return your completed Winter Jumble to us for a chance to win a $10.00 Gas Card. Ten winners will be drawn at random on February 13, 2015.

Fill out the information below and mail your completed Jumble to:

Winter Jumble
Carolina Disability Lawyers
802 41st Avenue South
North Myrtle Beach, SC 29582

Name: _____

Address: _____

_____

City: _____

State: _____

Zip: _____

Phone: _____

Winter Jumble

Find these winter words and activities in the jumble:

COLD
SNOWFLAKES
FREEZING
SCARVES
MITTENS
SLEDDING
ICE SKATING
SKIING
TOBOGGANS
HOCKEY STICK
GLOVES
SNOWSHOES
SHOVELING
BOOTS
WINTER COATS

```
C H L L I P I A J C O L D B U H O D N A
R M I S B U T K O R E V I S G L O V E S
H O C K E Y S T I C K I Z D Y G M C I I
D S E R F R A M E N I K B E M N W A F S
H E S V C A N Y V G A J O N I L I N R H
A W K H U S B O O T S E R A T O N V E R
G S A L G E R L P O D U F S T W T H E C
S K I W B T X I A R I T B T E K L I Z Z
H Y I V F I C Y E S D M H X N O R P I K
O I N A I S N O W F L A K E N X C E N I
V E G S I C U M A P G V C I I P O N G A
F P I D N A M H Z B R D U T G I A I W B
L E R F O R J L S K I I N G A R T L C R
I M A G U V O L I I W C O K H U S L M X
N I H N L E K S E R B I I P E W G N A F
G A P D V S N O W S H O E S S V I I J P
C S J G Y B I H A T I R N L E D D I N G
T O B O G G A N S G E T I C K M A H I B
```

About the Author

Ken Hardison practiced Injury and Disability Law for over 32 years and built one of the largest Personal Injury Law Firms in the state of North Carolina (www.LawyerNC.com). Ken currently has a Social Security Disability Firm (Carolina Disability Lawyers) in Myrtle Beach, SC (www.CarolinaSSDLawyers.com).

Ken attributes his success to his persistence and willingness to try new things, primarily in marketing. Ken has had proven success with his firm and in 2009 decided to share his knowledge with other lawyers. This led to the creation of PILMMA (Personal Injury Lawyers Marketing and Management Association). PILMMA is the only legal marketing and management association exclusively for Injury and Disability Lawyers.

Ken also co-founded Law Practice Advisor, an online marketing and management subscription service. Law Practice Advisor's purpose is to help all consumer lawyers grow their practices while living balanced lives.

Ken, a native of Dunn, North Carolina, graduated Cum Laude from Campbell University in 1979 and obtained his Juris Doctorate from Norman Adrian Wiggins School of Law in 1982.

Ken is the author of *How to Effectively Market Your Personal Injury Law Practice in the 21st Century* and *Under Promise, Over Deliver: How to Build the Preeminent Law Firm in Your Market,* along with numerous reports and articles about marketing and managing law firms. Ken is a sought-after speaker, legal coach, valued mentor and accomplished copywriter.

It has become Ken's mission to teach lawyers how to better market, manage and grow their practices through their involvement with PILMMA and Law Practice Advisor.

www.ingramcontent.com/pod-product-compliance
Lightning Source LLC
Chambersburg PA
CBHW071500200326
41519CB00019B/5807